English for GCSE

A Course for Further Education

Judith Baxter

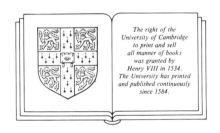

The right of the
University of Cambridge
to print and sell
all manner of books
was granted by
Henry VIII in 1534.
The University has printed
and published continuously
since 1584.

CAMBRIDGE UNIVERSITY PRESS

Cambridge
New York   New Rochelle
Melbourne   Sydney

Published by the Press Syndicate of the University of Cambridge
The Pitt Building, Trumpington Street, Cambridge CB2 1RP
32 East 57th Street, New York, NY 10022, USA
10 Stamford Road, Oakleigh, Melbourne 3166, Australia

© Cambridge University Press 1989

First published 1989

Printed in Great Britain by Scotprint, Musselburgh, Scotland

British Library cataloguing in publication data

Baxter, Judith
English for GCSE: a course for Further Education.
1. England. Further education. Curriculum subjects:
English language. G.C.S.E. examinations. Techniques
I. Title
420'.76

ISBN 0 521 35845 0

CE

ACKNOWLEDGEMENTS

The author and publisher would like to thank the following for permission to reproduce copyright material:

'A Life in the Day of Cilla Black' by Vivien Tomlinson from the *Sunday Times Magazine* (31.5.87), and 'She Wants to be Alone' by Russell Miller from the *Sunday Times Magazine* (20.7.86), © Times Newspapers Ltd, 1987, 1986. 'In Memory of My Grandfather' from *North Bank Night* by Edward Storey, published by Chatto and Windus, reprinted by permission of the author. Extract from *Teenage Romance or How to Die of Embarrassment* by Delia Ephron, with cartoons by Edward Koren, by permission of Victor Gollancz Ltd. Extract from *In My Own Name* by Sharan-Jeet Shan by permission of the Women's Press. 'Lonely Hearts' from *Making Cocoa for Kingsley Amis* by Wendy Cope, reprinted by permission of Faber and Faber Ltd. Extract from *Stags and Hens* by Willy Russell, by permission of Methuen London. Extract from *Portrait of the Artist as a Young Dog* by Dylan Thomas, published by Dent. Extract from *The Scarlet Thread* copyright © Rachel Barton 1987, published by Virago Press 1987. 'When the Tourists Flew In' from *Songs for the Unsung* by Cecil Rajendra, © 1983 World Council of Churches Publications. 'Request Stop' from *A Slight Ache and Other Plays* by Harold Pinter, by permission of Methuen London. Extract from *Part of My Soul* by Winnie Mandela (Penguin Books, 1985), copyright © Rowohlt Taschenbuch Verlag GmbH, 1984, reproduced by permission of Penguin Books Ltd. 'Prayer Before Birth' from *Collected Poems of Louis MacNeice*, reprinted by permission of Faber and Faber Ltd. 'The Windae Hingers' from *Stanley Baxter's Bedside Book of Glasgow Humour*, reprinted by permission of Constable Publishers Ltd. Extract from *Fraffly Suite* by Afferbeck Lauder, reprinted by permission of the author. 'No Dialects Please!' copyright Merle Collins, reprinted from *Watchers and Seekers*, ed. Rhonda Cobham and Merle Collins, The Women's Press 1986. 'Woman Work' copyright © *And Still I Rise* Maya Angelou 1978, published by Virago Press 1986. 'The Heroines' from *Dangerous Women* by Penny Windsor, published by Honno, Ailsa Craig, Heol y Cawl, Dinas Powys, South Glamorgan, CF6 4AH. Extract from *My Brilliant Career* by Miles Franklin is reproduced by permission of Angus and Robertson (UK). 'Science for Girls' from *Subject Options at School*, reprinted by permission of the Equal Opportunities Commission. 'The Equal Pay Act 1970' and 'The Sex Discrimination Act 1975' from *Rights, Responsibilities and the Law* by Judith Edmunds, reprinted by permission of Thomas Nelson and Sons Ltd. 'Input' by Bill Oddie, reprinted by permission of the author and the Guardian Newspapers Ltd. 'Meditation on the A30' from *Collected Poems* by John Betjeman, reprinted by permission of John Murray (Publishers) Ltd. 'The Fallen Birdman' by Roger McGough, reprinted by permission of A.D. Peters & Co. Ltd. 'A Man Was Killed' reprinted by permission of Mail Newspapers plc. 'Seven Deadly Myths about Nuclear Weapons', reprinted by permission of the Campaign for Nuclear Disarmament. 'Nato's Future at Stake', reprinted by permission of Families for Defence. 'The only class system . . .' advertisement, copyright The Receiver for the Metropolitan Police. 'Slimwheel' advertisement, copyright Leroco Ltd. 'The Earth life support system is failing' advertisement, reprinted by Friends of the Earth Trust Ltd. 'Hushed Puppies' advertisement, reprinted by permission of the Blue Cross Animal Welfare Society.

The author would also like to acknowledge all students whose work has been reproduced in this book.

Photographs are reproduced by permission of the following:
pp. viii, 3 David Cross; pp. 6–9, 21 David Runnacles; p. 13 Kim Sayer; p. 57 Kevin Cummins/Liverpool Playhouse; p. 64, 83(l) BBC Hulton Picture Library; p. 79, 81(l) Topham Picture Library; p. 81(r) Cecil Beaton/Camera Press London; p. 83(r) Curt Gunther/Camera Press London; p. 87(top) J. Allan Cash Photolibrary; p. 87(bottom) International Photobank; p. 90 Rex Features Ltd; p. 124 Kobal Collection; p. 125 Pat Mantle; p. 135 Crown Copyright, reproduced with the permission of the Controller of HMSO.

Illustrations by Amanda MacPhail.

Contents

To the teacher

This book is intended to help students in all forms of sixth year or further education, who are following a course in English such as GCSE, usually within one year. Many of these students may have already taken an English examination at school and are now hoping to achieve a higher grade. This book aims to help them achieve these practical expectations, while offering a learning approach to English which prepares their entry into young adulthood.

The teaching of English is concerned with developing the student's awareness and understanding of the possibilities of language use. This comes from recognising that the four language modes – reading, writing, speaking and listening – are interrelated and part of an interactive process between people. A student's ability to communicate effectively and appropriately will depend on the chance to explore and experiment widely with language. To this end, the book offers a range of stimulus material and opportunities in language work, as well as specific guidance in its use.

This is not intended to be a formal course book to be followed from start to finish. The stimulus material is organised into themes, from which choices can be made to appeal to the interests and needs of a particular group of students or to individual students. To a large extent the book encourages an attitude of 'self-help' – students should be able to read any section through on their own, in pairs or in groups and make decisions about the type of work they wish to do. However, the book has been designed for a year's course of study if required. So, to a certain extent, the thematic areas and the work requirements are graded in difficulty, both within each chapter and between successive chapters.

The approach to study in this book is based on course-assessment rather than on the examination. For this reason, there is less emphasis placed on the traditional written skills of comprehension, multiple choice, summary and composition than in some English textbooks. Instead, its focus is upon language as a process: that is, the process of carrying out exploratory language work in response to given stimulus material, leading on to more precisely defined and crafted work for oral performance or written presentation.

Guidance on language techniques is made part of this 'workshop' approach. The oral techniques of discussion and role play are considered to underlie so much English work that they are given a separate chapter (2). But the general principle in this book is that guidance on a language technique is offered in a chapter which requires its particular use. So, where students are asked to write a description in Chapter 3, a follow-on *Techniques* section in the same chapter offers guidelines on good practice in writing a description. (The *Contents* page is designed so that some cross-referencing in the use of the *Techniques* sections can take place.)

The material in this book is designed to meet the needs and interests of post-16 students. It has taken account of two areas of their personal development: their heightened sense of self and their relationships with people known and unknown; as well as their awakening responsiveness to life outside the self – to contemporary issues of an ideological and sometimes contentious nature. To reflect these interests, literary reading material in the book is drawn in the main from contemporary, recently published writing, which may be new to English textbooks. Non-literary material reflects as far as possible the range of ways in which language is used in a young person's life – especially its role in the mass media and as public information.

The work requirements in this book encourage students to respond in a variety of ways: on some occasions to be adventurous and experimental with language and on other occasions to be self-disciplined and precise – both sets of qualities vital to them as communicators in adult life. Some work activities are open-ended: that is, either of a creative, imaginative nature or of a critical, discursive nature drawing on a student's personal experience and response. Other activities are more 'closed': that is, case-study work involving one or more assignments based on close reading and comprehension. Here, the subject matter, form, audience and purpose are given and the assignments have specific objectives, requiring the use of particular language techniques.

It is hoped that this book will offer a stimulating and imaginative framework for a variety of teaching approaches. Teachers may use it for students of differing abilities, but will recognise themselves that suggested activities may be more appropriate for some students than for others. A teacher's guidance may therefore help students to select activities which both interest them and match their learning requirements. Whatever the choice of activity, its aim is to elicit a range of differentiated responses from students, whether singly, working with a partner or in a group.

1 A FRESH START

ICE-BREAKERS

A new college or school year is a difficult and challenging time. You may be joining a new class and meeting a large group of people for the first time. Even if you do know some people in the class, there will be other people you don't know. Added to this, you may well feel that after the long summer break, the classroom is an alien place.

If you have space to move around, try one or more of the following games and exercises. They work very well to 'break the ice' and help you to get to know new people.

1 How do you do?

The object of this exercise is to introduce yourself to as many people in your new class as possible in a given time (two minutes, perhaps).

When your teacher gives you the signal, move around quickly in the space available, introducing yourself, by shaking hands and giving your name to each new person you 'bump into'. Aim to meet everyone in the class by the time your teacher calls 'time!'.

2 Make friends/Argue

For this exercise pair off with someone you do not know. At the teacher's signal, begin to talk to each other, 'making friends'. Use this opportunity to find out about the other person. Carry on until you are told to freeze. Then begin talking in your pair again, but this time you must start an argument. After another 'freeze!', change your partner and repeat this process: making friends, then arguing. The teacher may spotlight one pair and ask them to continue their conversation for everyone else to listen to.

3 Observe closely!

(For this, you will need to be familiar with the names of everyone else in the class. Exercise 1 and 2 should have helped but play the Name Game (below) first, if there are still doubts.)

Have you got a good short-term memory? This exercise may help you to find out. As a class, walk around the room freely, each of you trying to take note of what people look like and are wearing. At the command 'freeze!', your teacher will spotlight two of you who happen to be back to back. If you are in this pair, you will be asked, in turn, to describe the person behind you as fully as possible. When both of you have given a description, you can then turn round and see how accurate you were.

Then as a class, move round the room again and repeat the process a few more times. So, observe closely!

If you do not have space to move around, try one or more of the following.

4 The name game

If you want to learn everyone's name in your new class quickly, there is probably no better way than this game.

The whole class should sit in a circle where it is possible to see everyone else. One person starts by turning to the person sitting on his left and says, 'My name's Paul; what's your name?' This person replies by giving her name. She then turns to whoever is sitting on *her* left and says, 'My name's Sue, this is Paul; what's your name?' Now you can probably guess the rest. The further round the circle you go, the more names each person must then memorise. So, the unfortunate person who goes last will have to recall the names of the whole class!

At the start of the next lesson, make sure you sit in the same places and try the game again. If you do this, you will be surprised at how many names you can remember!

5   Memory test

This exercise parallels 3 above, testing your powers of observation and memory. It probably works best with a fairly large group.

A volunteer is asked to leave the room for a couple of minutes. The volunteer should be assured that he or she will not be the victim of any tricks or surprises. Once the volunteer has gone out, try to recall as much as you can about the appearance of that person. Make courteous notes on the following: height, build, hair, skin and eye colouring, and clothes. Then, compare notes with a neighbour.

Now call the volunteer back into the room and see how accurate your notes and comparisons were. Perhaps 'honour' the volunteer with a few sample descriptions.

6   Interviews

(This exercise works best if you are a class of students who mostly do not know each other.)

Get to know someone else in the class a little better by following this exercise:

a   Sit beside someone you do not know very well – this is very important!

b   You will be given two minutes each, in turn. Decide which one of your pair will go first. Then, when the teacher gives the word, find out as much as possible about your partner: e.g. former school, where they live, age, family, courses opted for at college, hobbies and interests, musical tastes, impressions of the college so far, and so on.

c   When your teacher calls 'Stop!' after the allotted two minutes, swap over – the interviewer becomes the interviewee and vice versa. Repeat b in these new roles.

d   At the end of the second two minutes, you may be asked to recall to the class what you have learnt about your partner. Don't be too surprised if your memory fails to serve you well on this occasion!

7   Character reading

How much can you learn about someone by just looking at them? Is appearance a true indicator of character? Do we make snap judgements about people on first meeting them, which later turn out to be wrong? This exercise may give you some insight into the answers.

Sit beside someone you have not met before. Now do a character reading of this person. You already have their appearance, hairstyle and clothes style to go by, and you may have noticed the way they have behaved in previous exercises. Now make notes on what you guess to be their character, using the criteria below to help you:

Extrovert or introvert (Check you know the meaning of these terms.)
Hobbies/interests
Tastes in: fashion/music
Attitudes to study/politics
Favourite sports (if any)
Favourite entertainment
Horoscope sign.

When both of you have completed your notes, take turns to read out to each other your character assessment. When you have both done this, tell each other how accurate or inaccurate you were.

8 First impressions of the college

(This exercise clearly applies to those of you starting courses at a new college.)

You have given your first impressions of each other. Now consider what your impressions are of the college, both positive and negative.

One person in the class starts off: 'I like . . .' the next continues: 'But I don't like . . .' the next then says: 'I like . . .' and so on, with each person in the circle alternating with a positive then a negative impression.

9 Biography

Write a short biography of a person you have just met in your English class. The biography is to be a factual account of the main details of his or her life, rather than a character study.

a In pairs draw up some questions which will give each of you an overview of the other. Your biography will be written chronologically (that is, in a logical time sequence, from birth to young adulthood), so it may help to work out your questions accordingly. Questions might include: birthplace and date, places lived at, schools attended, family, hobbies and interests, job or career intentions.

b Now take turns to interview each other, jotting down all the main details as you proceed. Remember that neither of you need answer any question you do not wish to!

c Write up your notes as a biography, making sure that your account reads in a fluent and organised way.

A

B

6

C

D

E

_____
_____
_____
_____
_____
_____
_____
_____
_____
_____
_____

F

G

H

'A LIFE IN THE DAY OF . . . '

The next exercise continues the theme begun in the 'ice-breaking' exercises – our first impressions of people and how these impressions are formed. The exercise asks you to study photographs of people to see how much you can learn just by looking at a picture of their appearance. A photograph may give only one of many 'views' of a person, but it can give some insight into personality and social background.

The object of the exercise below is for you to use both the photographic evidence and your imagination to 'create' a character. You will find it helpful to study the sections on Role-play and Interviewing in chapter 2 for this.

1 Studying a photograph

In pairs, look closely at the photographs of people on the previous pages, and choose the one which interests you most. Then study the following features in the photograph and discuss what these may indicate about the mood, personality and/or social background of the person:

Appearance :	skin texture and colour
	hair texture, colour and style
	shape of eyes, nose, ears and mouth
	clothes: type and style
	make-up (if appropriate)
	accessories, e.g. pipe, jewelry, etc.
Expression :	how would you describe it?
	how posed or natural is it, for example?
	what does it tell you about the person?
Posture/Gesture :	(if visible on photo)
	how would you describe these?
	what do they tell you about the person?
Setting :	studio, home or outdoors?
	what does this tell you about the person?

2 Making judgements

Still in your pairs, now discuss and make notes on the following questions:

a   How old is the person in your photograph and how can you tell?
b   What type of work, if any, does the person do? Does the picture provide any clues to this?
c   What kind of social background does the person come from? How do you know this? Look particularly at details of appearance.
d   In your view, does the person live alone/with a partner/with a family?
e   What kind of personality does the person have? You can judge this

partly from the facial expression, attitude to the camera and the style
of hair and clothes.

f   How does the person speak? Think of dialect, regional accent, pitch
(high/low), and tone (quality of sound). (For further definitions, see
Techniques: 'Speaking English', chapter 6.)

g   What is the person called and where does he or she live?

When you have discussed the questions above, explain to the class the
views you have reached about the person in your photograph. If another
pair has studied the same photograph, you can then compare views and
how you reached them.

3 'A Life in the Day of . . . '

Now read the article on the next page about Cilla Black, from the feature
series in the *Sunday Times Magazine* on the life styles of people both
well-known and little known.

a   Why is the article called 'A Life in the Day of . . .' (instead of 'A Day in
the Life of . . .')?

b   In your pair, note down the various types of information you learn
about the person, e.g. eating habits, social life.

c   What are the clues in the article which show that Cilla Black was
interviewed first and then her commentary was 'written up' to read
like a diary extract?

4 Interview

Still in your pair, write (or improvise) an interview of the character you
have created from studying the person in your photograph. Imagine that
this is to be conducted by a *Sunday Times* journalist for the 'A Life in the
Day' series. Between you, decide which role each of you will play. Then,
when you have worked out the script of the interview, rehearse it, either
for 'live' performance before your class, or if you prefer, for audio-
cassette taping.

5 Article

Whether you were the journalist, or the person interviewed, write an
article based on your role-play, as if for publication in the *Sunday Times
Magazine*. Entitle it 'A Life in the Day of . . . (name of your character)'. Use
the article about Cilla Black as a model, as well as the material from the
interview script in order to write your own article.

A LIFE IN THE DAY OF

Cilla Black

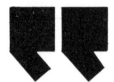 If it's a Monday morning I'll set my alarm for 7.30 to get the boys up and out for school. Other mornings our nanny Penny will do that and I'll get up about 8.30.

I'll just have tea or coffee and a piece of toast but the boys will have fruit juice and something different. Robert will have tomato ketchup on toast; Ben likes plain buttered bread spread with Bovril and Jack might have cheese and cucumber. Then our chauffeur will take Robert off to school in one direction while Bobby drives the younger two off in the other. Nobody thinks them anything special at school for being Cilla Black's sons. In fact we're probably at the bottom of the rung socially with all the oil magnates. I'm just a TV star, what's that?

Even so, my first thought in the morning is how lovely the house is – even after all these years. The boys, of course, have known nothing else. When we visited Bobby's brother in his three-up-three-down in Anfield the kids were fascinated, thought it was absolutely great. Everyone's front doors together. Millions of kids playing in the street. They wanted to know why we couldn't live somewhere like that. They step outside their own house and they've got nothing but 17 acres of grass and garden. It's the things Bobby and I wanted at their age but never thought we could have. But I once said we'd probably sell and move somewhere smaller when they were grown up. Robert was

horrified. He wanted to make me promise to let him buy it somehow and keep it in the family.

The kids have to be chauffered everywhere, but it's nice if they have friends round; they can all muck in and stay the night. There's no standing on ceremony. When I particularly appreciate the house is when our families come to stay. Me mam and Auntie Nellie are coming in a few weeks' time. The boys won't eat my scouse – I must be making it wrong – but they will eat my mother's.

We have a stable, regular, family routine wherever possible. I work more than six months every year on my television shows, *Surprise Surprise* and *Blind Date*, but that usually means only about two days a week at the studios. The rest is working from home with the production team coming here. People ask me why I still accept something like a summer show at Scarborough. They think I must be crazy. Well, I'm not. After all the television I need my fix of a live audience in an ordinary theatre. All I ever wanted to be remembered for anyway is as a singer.

When we come away for, say, a six-week season I have to arrange for the boys to be looked after, although we drive home after the Saturday night performance.

We have a marvellous nanny, Penny, who's been living with us 15 years. We have Tom and Margaret who live in the cottage in the grounds. Tom is the chauffeur/gardener and Margaret is housekeeper. They've been with us 12 years so it's all very settled.

But I am concerned for our boys' future. In the Sixties, when we were growing up, it was quite a boom. I was in the right place at the right time; I had a bit of talent but I was lucky. We've come from nothing. I had nowhere to go except up, being born where I was. We had a lot of love in our family but we could only ever be on a par or do better. We've given our children the best things we can – not money. We give them love and education and the benefit of our experience. They could be intimidated by our success but I don't think they will be. In any case they've been weaned on Cilla Black. When I come on the telly they just switch over. 'We've had enough of you in the house,' they say. 'We don't have to suffer you on the telly as well.'

At nine o'clock Margaret comes in and if it's a Monday she has to clear up the massacre of the weekend, what with the chaos made by the kids and our two Briard dogs, Hazel and Panza. I'm a fanatic about cleaning and on a Sunday morning I always go right through the house from top to bottom. I want the place to look its best. I think: 'What if the Queen dropped in and it was a real

Cilla Black, 44 last week, came to fame as a contemporary of the Beatles and, more recently, as a television personality. She was born and brought up in Liverpool's notorious Scotland Road area and married her childhood boyfriend, Bobby Willis, who is now her manager. They live in Buckinghamshire in an eight-bedroomed house with its own 17-acre estate. They have three sons, Robert, 16, Ben, 13, and Jack, who is 6.

tip?' Remember that time when the Queen was stuck in a snowstorm and dropped into someone's pub? Imagine that.

I don't have to clean during the week and if we're having a production meeting, well, I don't even have to make the coffee. One of the assistant stage managers will do that. And we'll send out for a take-away for everyone – a Chinese maybe. But by 2 o'clock they've all gone away and left me with the script. Bobby might take the dogs for a walk and I'll kick my shoes off and put my feet up to watch a tape or one of my favourite Australian television serials like *Sons and Daughters*.

The peace and quiet comes to an end around 3.30 when all hell breaks loose. Jack's the first home from school with a picture to show me and stories of what he's done at school. Then Ben's

home with Duran Duran going at full volume, or Madonna. Last it's Robert with Culture Club, the Beatles or even Bach. Yes, he's into that now. Robert wanted a Beatles album for his birthday. 'My God,' I told him. 'Help yourself. There's dozens up in the attic!' But they were no good. He wanted a special compilation.

I still see the Beatles. Ringo took us out to his gentlemen's club for dinner last Christmas. He asked if I'd mind if Paul and Linda came too. I had to say don't be so flash. Of course I didn't mind. In fact Paul did a most generous thing at the end of the meal. He nipped out to spend a penny and paid the bill. It's about two years since we bumped into George and his wife in a Chinese restaurant. He's so romantic, he bought all the ladies in our party carnations. Bobby seems to see Paul every Christmas at Cartier's. It sounds very posh but they do literally bump into each other. Mind you, Bobby has to put a suit and tie on. They let Paul in wearing his wellies and anorak, straight off the farm. There's real fame for you.

The younger children have their tea around 4.30. Robert, Penny and I will eat maybe steak and vegetables around seven. I try to eat low-fat foods but I still like my steak fried, and my onions in butter.

Often Bobby has been doing the kids' cooking so he won't feel like eating with us. He'll have a light meal later on. We do watch our weight. After my hysterectomy, when I had to take things easy, I started to put on a bit. Every morning I weigh myself. If I've put on even one pound I'll watch what I eat until it's back to normal. Bobby bought me a bike and I might take off round the estate on it some evenings with the boys hanging out of the windows laughing at me – or, even worse, following on their own bikes. I've also got weights and do a spot of training.

We're not great socialisers. As Bobby says, we know who we are and we don't have to go round telling people. We love people dropping in. They'll buzz at the gate, shout out who they are, and in they come. Jimmy Tarbuck might do that. Frankie Howerd comes on a Sunday sometimes and we stay up till four, talking.

When the boys are in bed or upstairs playing music we enjoy the evening together. At about 9.30 Bobby opens a bottle of champagne, yes, every evening, and we watch the telly.

I'm hardly ever in bed before one in the morning. Often it's later. I like my sleep, but can easily manage on six hours or less. Sleep on a clothes line, I can, and hardly ever need to read myself to sleep. Even if the Queen is dropping in tomorrow.

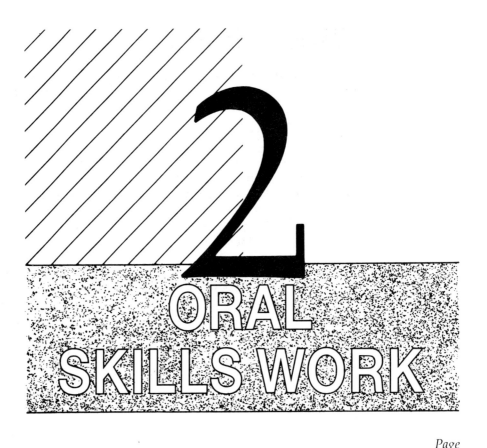

ORAL SKILLS WORK

DISCUSSION

This section looks at the reasons why discussion is an important part of an English course. It then gives some advice to help you improve your ability to discuss.

Why discuss?

Discussion is an essential oral skill in your English course. It used to be a very formal activity in the English lesson: a 'question-and-answer session' on a given subject conducted by the teacher with a few of the more outspoken pupils. The rest of the class would be, at best, silent listeners. Now that speaking and listening are assessed in most English courses, discussion is considered important for everybody. This is because it helps you to:
– check with others your understanding both of difficult concepts and the language used in what you hear and read;
– exchange views and ideas with others on controversial subjects;
– solve problems, make decisions and reach agreements with others;
– explore and express your ideas, thoughts and feelings;
– be more informed, confident and thoughtful in written work.

Exercise: *Qualities in a friend*

This exercise may help you to see some of the advantages *and* disadvantages of discussion. Also use it to consider how people need to behave in order to make a group discussion worthwhile.

a On your own, jot down 3–5 qualities which you think are important in a good friend.
b Now, as a class, pool your ideas so that your teacher can write up on the board ten qualities considered important in a friend.
c Again on your own, rank the ten qualities from 1 (for the best) to 10 in order of their merit, in your view.
d Now form into groups of about four, and in ten minutes aim to reach an agreement on a group ranking of the ten qualities. (Try to put across your reasons for ranking a particular quality high or low. In the end, though, you must be prepared for compromise to get a group agreement.)
e At the end of the exercise, elect a spokesperson to present the case for the group's ranking to the rest of the class.
f As a class, discuss your reactions to this exercise:
   – Did the group discussion help to give you a fuller view of the topic – qualities in a good friend – than you had on your own?
   – Did the discussion limit or exclude any ideas you may have had on your own?
   – From your own behaviour and observing other people's, what makes someone effective in a discussion?
   – What kind of behaviour makes someone ineffective?

How to be effective in discussion

How can you tell whether you are good (+) or bad (−) at discussion? This section considers which types of behaviour lead to both an effective and an ineffective discussion.

+   ## 1 Creating understanding

If you can create understanding with other people, you will certainly be effective in discussion. To do this, you should try to co-operate with each other, not compete against one another. If you can recognise the right of others to speak, this will encourage a greater range of ideas and views to be expressed. To create understanding towards others you should:

encourage : respond positively to the views, feelings and ideas of others even if you do not always agree with them. Ask quieter people to contribute their view.

relieve tension : ease negative feelings by humour or changing the angle of discussion.

−   ## Provoking tension

The opposite of creating understanding is provoking tension. This may happen if one person in the group is more concerned with his or her own ego than contributing to the discussion. Then other people in the group become tense and the chance of their contributing new and interesting ideas is reduced. A person who wants to cause tension tends to:

compete : vie with others to talk the most, impress the most.

be aggressive : assert themselves by criticising others.

fool around : refuse to take the activity seriously by clowning, joking, disrupting the group.

withdraw : act as if uninvolved by day-dreaming, doodling, etc.

+   ## 2 Good listening

If you are a good listener, you will understand others better. If a group listens carefully to each other, the discussion may be more effective because more points are heard and understood. Where agreement is needed at the end of a discussion, it is far more likely to be achieved if people listen to each other. Remember that good listening does not imply that you *have* to agree with each other! Instead, it helps people in a group to hear a range of ideas and opinions before final judgements are made. To be a good listener, use:

body language : show that you are listening by making eye contact with the speaker; nodding and perhaps smiling; neither fidgeting nor looking bored!

spoken language : acknowledge people's contributions; respond to their comments; try not to ignore and interrupt others.

Poor listening

If you are a poor listener in a discussion, you may have an ego problem! A person who doesn't listen is often one who doesn't try to understand other people or their point of view. A simple principle to remember is this: as you have two ears and one mouth, so you should listen to people twice as much as you speak. The signs of a poor listener are expressed in:

body language : avoiding eye contact, fidgeting, looking bored, yawning and so on.

spoken language : not listening to people, interrupting them and immediately disagreeing

3 Good speaking

To be a good speaker in a discussion, you need to be versatile: that is, be able to call upon a whole range of speaking approaches as appropriate. A good speaker will be able to:

give information, opinions and ideas.

seek information, opinions and ideas from others.

build : add to and support the ideas and points of others.

question assumptions : query the truth of something made to sound like absolute fact.

propose : suggest new ideas, new ways of looking at a topic, of defining a problem, or of reconciling differences between people in the group.

evaluate : be able to assess the strengths and weaknesses of your arguments and those of people who disagree with you.

summarise : your own case and those of others.

Poor speaking

There are two types of ineffective speakers in discussion: those who are shy and those who are self-centred! If you are fairly shy, you must make the most of discussion in pairs or small groups because practice will help you. Self-centred speakers tend to:

attack : be excessively critical of one person or point of view.

block : reject other people's arguments by talking over them; refuse to listen; argue stubbornly; or make negative remarks.

plead : express personal 'whines' and pet concerns unrelated to the group's activities.

take over : interrupt a person talking, then 'take over' the point being discussed.

Exercise: *Job Values*

How effective do you think you are in a discussion? The following exercise involves you in two simultaneous activities – a group problem-solving exercise and an assessment by an observer of your skills in discussion.

The group

1   Form into groups of about six and then appoint from the group a non-participating observer. (See *The observer*.)

2   Each person in your group is given a card which has written on it *one* of the following occupations:

Miner	*Doctor*
Social worker	*Hairdresser*
Computer programmer	*Shopkeeper*
Farmer	

Also look at the photographs on p. 21.
Next, your group is 'given' a fictional sum of money (say, £850 for 5 people). The object of the exercise is for the group to reach a decision on how to share out this amount as a weekly wage to each occupation. This decision will obviously depend on the group's views of the worth of each occupation. However, you will be expected to 'fight' for the occupation on your own card in order to win as high a share of the total sum as you can reasonably argue for.

3   Before starting the discussion, spend five minutes on your own working out a case for the worth of the occupation on your card.

4   As a group, you have about twenty minutes both to present the case for the worth of each job and to come to an agreement, with reasons, about how the money should be allocated.

5   Appoint a spokesperson (not the observer), to present the group's decision to the class, e.g. 'We felt that the miners should get the most because . . .'

6   Lastly, as a class, compare and contrast the values implied in each group's decisions about how to distribute money to the various occupations. For example, which group was the most egalitarian – that is, wanting equal recognition of different jobs? Which was the most hierarchical – that is, wanting graded distinctions between different jobs?

The observer

Your job is to watch the way each person in the group behaves in the discussion and to record your observations on a copy of the *Assessment Sheet* (see the next page). As observer, you need to be familiar with the qualities described above which make people good or bad in discussion. To record your observations, tick the appropriate box on the chart each time a person displays one of the listed features. As you go along, you will notice a pattern of behaviour emerging for each person in your group. At the end of your observation, put *x* in boxes where a type of behaviour is *not* true of that person at all.

When the exercise has finished, tell your group what your findings are. Try to give each person a detailed idea of his or her strengths and weaknesses in discussion. Also, from your observation of the group, assess how successful it was in resolving the problem set in the exercise.

Reflection

What have you learnt about your strengths and weaknesses in discussion?

Did any of the observer's comments surprise you? What can you try to do to improve your performance in future group discussions?

If your group failed to reach an agreement in the *Job Values* exercise, was this because people in the group did not discuss things very well? Conversely, if your group did come to an agreement, was this because each person discussed the problems well?

Assessment Sheet

Date:	Activity:
Group:	Observer:

Names

(+)

Creating understanding						
Good listening						
Giving information						
Seeking information						
Building						
Questioning assumptions						
Proposing						
Evaluating						
Summarising						

(−)

Provoking tension						
Poor listening						
Attacking						
Blocking						
Pleading						
Taking over						

(+) *Effective discussion*   (−) *Ineffective discussion*

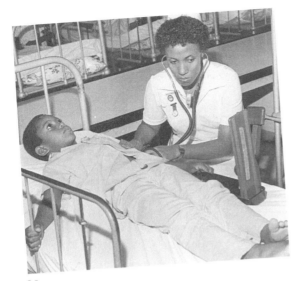

Nurse

Cook

Mechanic

Police Officer

21

INTERVIEWING

*This section looks at the skills you need to interview someone effectively. It will help you in your work both for the 'A Life in the Day' exercises in chapter 1 and for interviewing work throughout this textbook. The section does not advise specifically on the skills you need when you are **being** interviewed, as these may depend on the particular situation. Being interviewed often requires playing a role both in English work and in real life. So, the third part of this chapter looks at skills in role-play.*

Why interview?

Interviews are conducted for two main reasons:

1 *Interest and entertainment* : for example a TV/Radio/Magazine interview with a 'personality'. Here, the main purpose is to encourage the person interviewed to talk freely, revealing something of their experiences and personality to an audience.

2 *Information* : for example a job interview; consumer survey; court case or police investigation of a crime. The main purpose here is to find out specific things from a person, which may then be acted upon.

Some interviews may be held for both reasons. Can you think of any examples?

Interviewing skills

Interviewing requires special skills. Whatever the reason for the interview, the aim is to get your interviewee to tell you what you wish to know. This may be simply to reveal their personality – or it may be to learn a biographical fact about them. Consider why different types of interview require differing approaches.
– Why, for example, might a police officer interrogating a suspected criminal deliberately make this person feel tense and on edge?
– Why do you think that in many types of interview it is best to encourage the person interviewed to feel relaxed and at ease?

Good questioning

To be a good interviewer you need to be able to ask the right questions and listen well to the answers. Knowing which type of question to ask a person will help you to find out what you wish to know about them.

If you want to encourage your interviewee to talk freely, then the following question types may help them to relax:

1 *Open-ended* : This allows the interviewee freedom in answering.

  e.g. 'Tell me about yourself . . .'
    'What are you feelings about . . . ?'

2 *Mirror* : This shows you are listening and understanding by mirroring the wording of an answer.

  e.g. 'So, are you really saying that . . . ?'
    'In other words . . .'

3 *Hypothetical* : This enables the interviewee to think through a practical situation.

  e.g. 'Suppose you were to do it this way . . .'

4 *Prompting* : This helps the interviewee with a mental block or when he or she does not know how to answer the question.

  e.g. 'Tell me about your work experience . . . for example, what did you do last summer?'

If the main purpose of the interview is to find out specific things, then the following question types may be more appropriate:

5 *Close-ended* : This allows your interviewee little freedom of response.

  e.g. 'How long were you an actress?'

6 *Yes/no* : There are (more or less) two possible answers and again this restricts the freedom of reply.

  e.g. 'Do you like living alone?'

7 *Loaded/leading* : This makes it very obvious what the answer has to be.

  e.g. 'Do you believe in all this nonsense about . . . ?'

8 *Probing* : This probes an interviewee's answer to get more information.

  e.g. 'Could you give me an example of that point?'

Good listening

An interviewer who is a good listener will encourage the interviewee to relax and speak freely. Most people like to be listened to, if only they are given the chance! You can show that you are a good listener in two ways:

Body language

Body language often indicates far more about your attitude to somebody than what you say. If you wish to encourage your interviewee to feel at ease and to talk fully, then there are ways you can do this without saying a word.

1 *Eye contact* : Looking an interviewee in the eye as he or she speaks, shows that you are listening. Obviously, if you stare continuously at them, you will look threatening and put them off! Conversely, if you are looking out of the window or around the room as they are talking, you will appear bored and distracted. Your interviewee may then stop talking altogether.

2 *Expressions* : Looking interested by smiling and nodding your head occasionally encourages an interviewee to feel relaxed. They are more likely to develop a point if they are getting encouraging signals from you. If you are frowning, yawning, shaking your head or looking blank, you will certainly put your interviewee off.

3 *Gestures* : Smooth, sweeping hand movements when you are asking a question encourages talk. Aggressive or restless movements such as finger jabbing, fidgeting, playing with a pencil, scratching or pulling your own hair, nose or ears indicate boredom or impatience.

Spoken response

Your spoken response to what an interviewee has to say is also important. You have the power either to encourage them to speak further or to make them 'close off'. Here are some of the common ways of responding.

1 *Encouraging* : These are signs that you are listening and understanding.

> e.g. 'I see . . .'
> 'That's interesting . . .'
> 'Uh-huh.'

Examples of off-putting and discouraging remarks are:
> 'No . . . no, I don't agree at all . . .'
> 'Surely not . . .'

2 *Restating* : This is where you show a wish to understand by restating points.

> e.g. 'So what you're saying is . . .'
> 'In other words you think . . .'

There is a danger that you may have misinterpreted what the interviewee has said, but this response usually encourages clearer talk.

3 *Reflecting* : Here, you reflect the person's feelings and indicate some sympathy.

> e.g. 'So you feel strongly that . . .'
> 'You must have been very upset when . . .'

If you wanted to provoke the person, you might disagree with what they are saying by replying with loaded questions or comments:
> 'Surely you can't agree with the view that . . .'

Exercises

1 Using different question types

In pairs, choose one of the following subjects and make up a set of questions drawing on all 8 question types on p. 23:

> *Christmas* – questions to Santa Claus.
> *Personality profile* – questions to a pop-star, sports or TV personality of your choice.
> *Issue of the day* – questions to a politician.

Then read the questions out to another pair. See if they can guess each question type used.

2 Using different interview approaches

a Again in pairs, choose *one* of these two interview approaches:
   - the interviewer deliberately provokes and upsets the interviewee;
   - the interviewer is encouraging and supportive.

   Use your approach in *one* of the following situations:
   - TV interview of a politican
   - Police interview of a suspected criminal
   - Police interview of a victim of a crime
   - Job interview
   - A TV interview with a famous 'personality'
   - An interview in a TV commercial: e.g. soap powder, cat food.
b In your pair, decide who will be the interviewer and who the interviewee. Prepare the interview together, drawing on appropriate question types, body language and spoken response to indicate the interview approach. Then rehearse it.
c Take turns to present your interview to the class. Let the class comment on how effectively you have conveyed your interview approach.

ROLE-PLAY

This last section gives you some guidelines about role-play. English work often requires you to imagine being someone else, or to imagine that you have different feelings and attitudes from your own. This is to help you broaden your own experience of life, by understanding other people's views and experiences. These guidelines should help you with some of the role-play exercises in this book.

Role-play is similar to acting. The main difference is that in role-play you often improvise – that is, create for yourself what you are going to say and do; in acting, you usually learn the lines of someone else's script. The main similarity is that you become someone else, by taking on a role.

Think of an actor or actress you admire in a current television serial. One of the qualities which makes them good is that they seem to *become* the character they are acting. It is unlikely that, in real life, they will speak or behave in the way they do in the serial, yet many popular actors and actresses get fan mail from people who really believe they *are* the people they play! Their skill is to role-play so well that they walk, talk, behave and even appear to think like the characters they are playing.

To be a good role-player, like a good actor, you have to 'get into' the skin and mind of the person you are playing.

To do this, think of seven things:

1 *What is their background?*
   e.g. – education?
         – job or career?
         – family life and personal relationships?
         – how poor or wealthy?
         – how successful or unsuccessful?
         – main interests in life?

2 *What are they like as people?*
   e.g. – reserved/confident?
         – humourless/witty?
         – rude/polite?
         – cold/warm-hearted?

3 *What events may have affected their lives?*
   e.g. – love; marriage; divorce?
         – loss of someone close?
         – getting/losing a job?
         – public success or failure?
         – a physical addiction: to alcohol, etc.?
         – an accident or illness?

4 *What attitudes and beliefs do they hold?*
   e.g. – towards other people: competitive or co-operative?
         – towards themselves: how satisfied/dissatisfied?
         – towards politics, changes in our society, etc.?
         – towards religion: a particular faith?

5 *How do they speak?*

   e.g. – softly/loudly?
   – slowly/quickly?
   – shyly/confidently?
   – clearly/unclearly?
   – wittily/humourlessly?
   – with a particular dialect or accent?

6 *How do they dress?*

   e.g. – formally/casually?
   – expensively/according to their means?
   – fashionably/unfashionably?
   – smartly/untidily?

7 *What body language is typical of them?*

   e.g. – gestures : quick/slow?
                     relaxed/nervous?
                     enthusiastic/bored?
   – expressions : how much eye contact?
                           calm/restless?
                           changing/constant?
   – posture : upright/slumped?
                    relaxed/restless?
                    dignified/ungainly?

Use this checklist when you are preparing to role-play a character, such as for the 'A Life in the Day' interview in chapter 1. Interviews require a detailed character sketch, so all seven questions above will be useful. For some role-plays though, you may only need to give a superficial character sketch. In these cases, concentrate on making decisions about *the way the character behaves* (questions 2, 5, 6, 7).

Exercise

In pairs, think of an actor or actress you both admire, perhaps in a current television serial or recent film. Use the checklist above to analyse how they have 'composed' the role they play. That is, discuss which decisions the actor/actress has made in creating the character you watch on the screen.

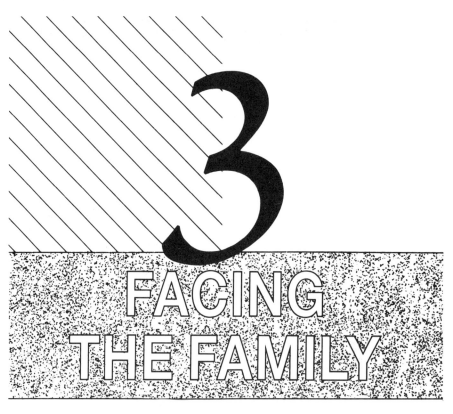

3

FACING THE FAMILY

DESCRIBING YOUR FAMILY

Poems by students

Mum

Mum,
plump, pink
heaving, sighing, puffing,
fights the flab at keep fit,
Mum.

Jane

Tom

Tom,
lean, earringed,
swearing, shouting, cheering,
never as tough as he looks,
Tom.

Anne

Sue

Sue,
surly, sleek
sulking, mocking, smirking,
moon eyes at waiters,
Sue.

John

Dad

Dad,
cross, canine,
barking, snapping, baying,
always touchy at breakfast,
Dad.

Moira

My Brother Paul

Paul is sitting in my favourite armchair. I thought how absolutely typical this was of him. He only sat there to annoy me. He did many things which made me angry, but being Paul he always got away with them. I sat watching him. He is only fourteen but could easily be mistaken for sixteen by anyone who does not know him. His face is handsome. His eyes, large and hazel, sparkle with alertness. They are framed with long, dark lashes giving them the resemblance of a young calf's eyes. His cute, button nose, covered in freckles, twitches in characteristic fashion. Paul's short, brown hair, shaped round his face, enhances his good looks now, but does nothing for him first thing in the morning. It has a handy way of sticking out at every angle, which makes him look like a scarecrow. He is very fastidious about his hair and will spend a long time in the bathroom trying to flatten it with water. If his hair does not comply with his wishes the world is hit with one of the moodiest people around.

Although only fourteen, Paul is very mature. He has a dark moustache which makes him look very sexy and tough. As this would embarrass him, I would never tell him so. He is self conscious of his early development as very few of his friends have fully matured. As he stands up the full extent of his development is seen. He has the typical male shape already of wide shoulders and narrow waist. His arms are like iron due to the hard muscles which he has built up through weight training. His body is absolutely free of any fatty tissue. He is pure muscle. This can only be from all the sport he does. Although he slouches when he is sitting down, Paul walks with the straightness of an athlete. He does not have the annoying habit of putting one hand in his trouser pocket and walking along, as so many men do.

When at home, Paul is a fairly cordial person, but as soon as he meets up with his friends, his personality changes. He becomes lively and full of teenage madness. In the company of our parents, he is evasive and shy about his attitude towards girls. Dad teases him about them, which he reacts to with annoyance, which is really embarrassment. His nose and cheeks turn bright red when he becomes embarrassed. It makes him look funny and I cannot help but laugh, which only makes him worse.

Paul got up from my armchair. He was clutching school books. I looked at him closely. He meticulously set out his pens, pencils and books on the table in front of him. Then he sat with his head in his hands, just looking at the books. After a few minutes he groaned; he always groaned before starting his homework, and then proceeded to write as quickly as he could. From this I guessed he was doing some French work. This being his least favourite subject, he does it as quickly and as untidily as possible. After a few minutes of mad scribbling he put down his pen and looked at me with his own cheeky grin, which brought dimples to his face. Needless to say, I ended up doing his French as I always do, while Paul sat back and watched television. As to many other things Paul had taken the easy way out of something he could not do. I know I should not have done the work, but I can rarely refuse him anything, he is far too good at charming people.

a student

In Memory of My Grandfather

Swearing about the weather he walked in
like an old tree and sat down;
his beard charred with tobacco, his voice
rough as the bark of his cracked hands.

Whenever he came it was the wrong time.
Roots spread over the hearth, tripped
whoever tried to move about the room;
the house was cramped with only furniture.

But I was glad of his coming. Only
through him could I breathe in the sun
and smell of fields. His clothes reeked
of the soil and the world outside;

geese and cows were the colour he made them,
he knew the language of birds and brought them
singing out of his beard, alive
to my blankets. He was winter and harvest.

Plums shone in his eyes when he rambled
of orchards. With giant thumbs he'd split
an apple through the core, and juice
flowed from his ripe, uncultured mouth.

Then, hearing the room clock chime,
he walked from my ceiling of farmyards
and returned to his forest of thunder;
the house regained silence and corners.

Slumped there in my summerless season
I longed for his rough hands and words
to break the restrictions of my bed
to burst like a tree from my four walls.

But there was no chance again of miming
his habits or language. Only now,
years later in a cramped city, can I
be grateful for his influence and love.

Edward Storey

Poems by students

Writing a poem

See if you can write a poem using the same approach as those at the beginning of the chapter, in which you describe a member of your family, or a person you know really well. The aim here is to select describing words to convey appearance, actions and behaviour, which capture some of the essential characteristics of your person.

Here is a reminder of the poem's pattern. (Each line represents a word.)

My Brother Paul

Discussion

Read the description 'My Brother Paul' carefully, and then discuss the following questions:

a   Which features of the description work well in portraying Paul, in your view?

b   How has the writer avoided making the description read like a list of points in answer to the exercise below?

c   Which features of the description do you feel work less well?

d   Can you detect where the style changes from description to 'telling a story' (that is, a narrative approach)?

Do you feel that this change of style adds to or detracts from the description of the writer's brother?

Now try the following exercise to help you write your own description. You may find it useful to refer to *Techniques*: 'Describing People' for extra guidance.

Describing people

Watch a member of your family or a close friend when they are doing something absolutely familiar to them – for example: watching the television, washing up, sleeping in an armchair, doing homework, eating a meal. Then make notes on some or all of the following aspects of your selected person's physical make-up and personality. Try to use descriptive words which convey as convincingly as possible the nature of your person:

a	Facial features :	Eyes, nose, mouth, hair, peculiar characteristic features: e.g. glasses (and the way they are worn), balding head, make-up, beard/moustache, haircut. NB. Notice the things they are really fussy about! Also their reactions to their own appearance: – are they self-conscious, embarrassed, vain? – how can you tell?
b	Physique :	Size, height, shape of body, attitude to their body, characteristic bodily movements.
c	Clothes :	Taste in clothes; what clothes mean to them. Imply your opinion, 'When he wears a sweat-shirt it really suits him, but when he wears . . .' How aware of fashion is the person? Be honest!
d	Mannerisms :	Characteristic fidgets, twitches, gestures, habits, movements. Your reactions to these.
e	Behaviour with people :	How differently does the person behave with: members of the family, friends, strangers?
f	Voice/speech :	Note accent, dialect, tone, use of stresses, favourite words and expressions.
g	My relationship with this person :	Feelings and reactions; areas of agreement and disagreement between you; what charms and attracts you; what embarrasses, irritates or annoys you.

When you have completed your notes, use these to write a vivid descriptive 'portrait' of your person.

In Memory of My Grandfather

Appreciating a poem

Read the poem through carefully at least twice, including one reading aloud. Then discuss the answers to the following:

a Why did Edward Storey, as a child, look forward to his grandfather's visits so much?

b How can we tell that the house is not the grandfather's natural environment? Pick out phrases or lines in answer to this and explain them.

c How does the poet make his grandfather sound larger than life? Discuss the use of any phrases or lines which suggest this.

For a closer study of the poem's use of language, read *Techniques*: 'Describing People', and answer the questions there.

Describing people

Descriptive writing gives an idea of what a person, place or thing is like, or used to be like. It works by creating a picture in words: our imagination is stimulated by the verbal picture so that we can then visualise and perhaps sense the described subject.

To describe vividly either a person you know or a fictitious character, try following this guidance:

1 Selected detail

In order to describe a person's individual nature, select only those aspects of appearance, behaviour and personality which both typify them and bring them to life.

In 'In Memory of My Grandfather', we are not given a photographic impression or a detailed character study of the old man. Yet we sense strongly the central quality about the poet's grandfather – his oneness with nature.

- Find three phrases in the poem which suggest this oneness with nature. Then explain *how* each phrase suggests this.

2 Concrete detail

If you wish to make the described person seem real and alive to your reader, refer to essential and distinguishing details about them. In 'My Brother Paul', it is important that we know he has a 'dark moustache' as this conveys that he is making the transition from boyhood to manhood.

- In 'In Memory of My Grandfather', what are the various things we learn about the grandfather's nature in the following lines?

  > *With giant thumbs, he'd split*
  > *an apple through the core,*

  and: *He was winter and harvest.*

3 The senses

Another way of making a person seem real in the imagination of your readers is to stimulate their senses by referring to colours and shapes, to sounds, textures, smells and perhaps tastes.

'In Memory of My Grandfather' evokes several of our five senses to the extent that we can almost feel the old man's strong, physical presence in the way that his grandson did. Colours are not evoked explicitly, but the references to natural objects – to trees, sun, soil, plums and apples – create a sense of colourful contrasts. Sounds, smells and touch (textures), however, *are* evoked explicitly.

- Find examples from the poem where each of these three senses are strongly suggested.

4 Vivid vocabulary

Try to use words which convey a strong sense of the person described but which are as precise as possible.

For example, words like 'thin' or 'fat' are really generalisations. More precise words for 'thin', depending on the context, are: gaunt, elfin, lean, wiry, diminutive, spare, slight, and so on. For 'fat', alternative words include: stout, portly, corpulent, burly, stalwart, brawny, ample, capacious.

Use a thesaurus to help you widen your vocabulary and to choose less obvious and more precise descriptive words. But take care! Avoid using clever sounding words for their own sake – the effect can be worse than the original word you rejected.

5 Comparisons

Descriptive writing makes particular use of comparison. This technique is known as 'imagery' or 'figurative writing'. There are two types of comparison, of which you are likely to have heard:

Simile is where one thing is compared to something else, using the words 'like' or 'as' to join the two halves of the comparison.

> *. . . makes him look* like *a scarecrow* ('My Brother Paul')

Here, Paul's untidy hair is compared to the straw hair of a scarecrow.

> *his voice, rough* as *the bark of his cracked hands*
> ('In Memory of My Grandfather')

In this quotation, the roughness of the old man's voice is compared to both a tree's bark and to his hands roughened by work.

- Find one further example of simile in the poem and explain the significance of the comparison.

Metaphor is where one thing *is* another thing. There are no link words to join the two halves of the comparison.

> *button nose* ('My Brother Paul')

Paul's nose is not really a button but it looks like one. A simile would read: 'His nose was like a button', or 'His nose was as small and round as a button' – the comparison is made much more explicit.

- Find at least five uses of metaphor in the poem and try to explain the significance of each comparison. (For example, 'Plums shone in his eyes . . .' The grandfather's eyes shine with colour and health in the way that ripe plums do.)

FAMILY RELATIONSHIPS

HOW TO TALK TO YOUR MOTHER

You are about to leave the house:
'Where are you going?'
'Out.'
'Out where?'
'Just out.'
'Who are you going with?'
'A friend'
'Which friend?'
'Mom, just a friend, okay? Do you have to know everything?'
'I don't have to know everything. I just want to know who you're going out with.'
'Debby, okay?'
'Do I know Debby?'
'She's just a friend, okay?'
'Well, where are you going?'
'Out.'

———————

You have just come home:
'Hi, Mom, did anyone call?'
'You did get one call, but I forgot to ask who it was.'
'Male or female?'
'Male.'

'And you didn't ask! Thanks. Mom, thanks a lot, I really appreciate it. For all I know it was the most important phone call of my life!'

———————

You have just hung up the telephone:
'Who was that, dear?'
'Can't a person have some privacy once in a while!'

———————

You are having a party Saturday night. Your mother has just announced that she expects the guests to stay out of the bedrooms:
'Why?'
'I'd just prefer it.'
'Why don't you say it, Mom – SEX. You think everytime two people walk into a room and close the door they're having sexual intercourse. That's what you think, isn't it? Honestly, it's totally ridiculous.'
'It's not that, it's –'
'You don't trust me.'
'That's not true.'
'You don't. You don't trust me. How do you think that makes me feel?' Look her straight in the eye. 'Mom, you have my word – nothing is going to happen.'
'I'm sorry, I can't allow it.'
'Can't allow it.' Can't allow it!!! It's my house too, you know, I live here. I have rights! You really don't trust me, that's what it's about, isn't it, you don't trust me. That's terrible. You don't even trust your own kid. God, I don't believe it – a mother who doesn't trust her own kid. Just think about that, Mom, just think about it.'

———————

Your mother has just put dinner on the table.
'Oh, Mom, I meant to tell you, I'm a vegetarian.'

Walk into the house, go to your room, close the door, and turn on the stereo. Your mother knocks:

'Hi, where've you been?'

You do not answer. Fiddle with the stereo, adjusting the balance.

'Would you turn that down while I am trying to talk to you?'

Turn it down, very slightly.

'I said. "Turn the music down"!'

Shut it off. Cross your arms in front of your chest, and exhale loudly, appearing exasperated and bored at the same time. "Yes."

'Whenever I try to talk to you, you're busy. You just come home to eat and sleep. You treat this house like a hotel. Would it be too much trouble, when you arrive home, to come in and say hello?'

'Hello. Now are you satisfied?'

———

You and your mother are at the movies. Your mother thinks something that just happened on the screen is very funny:

'Mom, cut it out, stop laughing so loud. Everyone's looking.'

———

It's Saturday night and your mother is insisting that you be home by midnight:

'Oh, Mom, come on. Nobody gets home that early, nobody! Do you want me to be the only kid in the entire group that has to leave early! The only one who can't stay out! Do you? Do you want me to ruin everyone else's time because I have to leave because my mom doesn't trust me while everyone else's mom does? Is that what you want? Is it? Great, just great. You're really getting impossible, you know that? You've changed, Mom, you have. You never listen, you never try to understand. You just give orders – do this, do that. This isn't the army, you know. You're not my boss!'

'Until you're eighteen years old, I am your boss whether you like it or not.'

'Oh, Mom, come on, just this once. Please. Pretty please. I never have any fun. I really don't. You never let me do anything I want. Never. If you had your way, I'd be in jail. You know, you're ruining my life. Probably no one will ever invite me anywhere again as long as I live. I'll probably never have another date. I'll spend the rest of my life in my room. Is that what you want? Is it? I hope you're happy, I really hope so. Maybe I won't even go. I mean, what's the point? I have to come home before the party's even started.'

———

Your mother went out for dinner. She has just returned home:

'Hi, Mom, how was the food?'

'Gross.'

'Oh Mom, stop trying to act cool.'

———

You have just returned from school.

'How'd you do on the science test?'

'Can't you ever stop asking me questions!'

'I really think that's uncalled for. If I ask, you tell me I'm prying. If I don't ask, you say I'm not interested. I can't win.'

'That's right, Mom, you can't.'

Delia Ephron from *Teenage Romance*
or *How to Die of Embarrassment*
with drawings by Edward Koren

Param-Jeet Runs Away from Home

In the following passage from her autobiography, Sharan-Jeet Shan describes an incident in her life, at the age of sixteen, when her brother, Param-Jeet decides to leave home. The effect upon her family is a terrifying one.

Param-Jeet did not have any special interests. My father had very special dreams for him as he was the only son and, regardless of his capabilities, he was expected to realise those dreams. When the time came, he was to sit the entrance examination for the National Defence Academy at Kharkwasla, Poona, pass it and train there as an army officer. To help him achieve this, I used to do a lot a research into the nature of the tests he was to sit. I had taken over that responsibility as Babuji was always busy with various duties at his office. Besides, he had no patience with Param-Jeet. If Param-Jeet did not grasp any academic fact, it was always put down to laziness and lack of effort rather than of ability. In my father's view, non-achievement had to be punished. After all, he himself had done brilliantly at school and college. And why should I have learnt everything with such ease and not Param-Jeet?

The only punishment, the only retributive measure he knew was the stick. Param-Jeet was fourteen now. Resentment about this physical punishment was building up inside him. He had talked often about running away to Bombay and becoming an actor. I had heard him and Achal (Param-Jeet's closest friend and our next door neighbour) talk about it seriously. They had told me of their plan and had made me take an oath that I would not tell their secret to anyone. I was to ask Babuji for some money to buy a couple of new books for English literature; I must convince him that if he wanted me to secure first place in that year's finals, studying the two books was absolutely imperative. Then I was to give that money to Param-Jeet. It was what my English friends would call Hobson's Choice. If I said no, Param-Jeet would get angry at me, threaten not to eat or generally tell lies about me to our mother, who would be after me with a stick. If I said yes, I would have to face the most awesome consequences. There was no escape from this emotional blackmail. How was I going to explain to my father yet again about losing money? I was getting desperately tired of explaining the foolhardiness of his scheme to Param-Jeet. I wanted to run away with him to avoid the traumatic emotional drama that would follow in our household. And what about the effect such an impetuous action would have on our mother? I had read about the psychological effects of sudden shocks on people, particularly those with a predisposition to depression. What if Mother were to lose her mind or her speech or sustain some such permanent impediment? Param-Jeet was her only son. She already had very little standing in my father's family. If she were to lose Param-Jeet, her whole world would shatter. No, I could not let Param-Jeet run away. Besides, how would he protect himself against all those odds, natural and man-made? Bombay was one of the most corrupt cities in the world. I had heard of children being made into cripples and used for begging. I tried to argue, begged him to let me go with him, but to no avail. He kept defending his decision and told me that if I wanted to be a good, kind *didi* (older sister), I would let him go. He simply could not take Babuji's nagging and beating any more. He was going to run away, come what may.

The following day, I came home from school to find that Param-Jeet had gone. I tiptoed into my bedroom to find a note he was supposed to have left for Mother. There was no note, no letter. Mother had not realised that anything was wrong. I went on to the verandah. *Charpais* (Indian beds) were stacked neatly against the wall. I pulled one down and tried to go to sleep, but my heart-beat was so loud, it was almost deafening me. I could not sit still. I went into the kitchen to get some water. As usual, Mother was preparing the meal. She told me to get the plates ready and wait for Param-Jeet to come. She made some remark about him being late. I could not hide my anxiety and fear any more. Uncontrollable tears and sobs just burst from me. 'He has left home, Mother.' I tried to sound casual. 'He only wanted to teach Babuji a lesson. He will be back in a week or two, he promised.'

Mother looked at me. Her deep-set eyes seemed devoid of all life. Her lower lip started to tremble and she went as white as a sheet. I remember thinking, 'Oh God! She is going to faint. Maybe even die!' Instead, like lightning, her right hand fell across my face with all the force she could muster.

'Hold your tongue. Aren't you ashamed, talking about your brother like that?' Then, after a short restless pause she started shouting at me, tears streaming down her face, in uncontrollable hysterics. 'Why didn't you tell me if you knew? You wanted him to go. You wanted him to run away. You are his enemy. You have an only brother. A sister should cherish her only brother. Sisters all over the world do, but not you. Oh no!' And then she started hitting her head against the kitchen wall.

'You are *parai* [someone else's property]. You are a *mehman* (guest). If he does not come back, I shall have no place to hide. *Hai Rab* (Oh God)! I want to die.'

I recalled that the mother of an only son is like a blind person; the only son is like the guiding stick. Without the son, she would have no cause left to live. 'Oh Mother, you have me. I love you and care for you too. I would never have run away and caused you such suffering,' I pleaded from a distance. I wanted to put my arms around her, to comfort her.

I pulled at her *kurta* [shirt], trying to stop her. She picked up the rolling pin and threw it at me. Then she sat down and started beating her chest and head with clenched fists, making a fearful sound all the time. I stood there crying, hoping for a miracle to occur, helpless, not knowing how to comfort my mother. I must have seemed like the devil incarnate to her. I wanted to go. I had barely reached the door when Mother got up, made a dash for my hair, dragged me back and started slapping me.

'You know where he has gone? Tell me then! Why don't you speak? Isn't there a tongue in your mouth?'

My tears and promises of truthfulness and honesty did not convince her.

Sharan-Jeet Shan
from *In My Own Name*

Causes of Friction

Young people have a strong tendency to resist authority and therefore often want to do the opposite of what they are asked. This is tied up with their desire to be recognised as individuals and their breaking loose from shackles. They want to choose their own friends, amusements, clothes and books. The parents' reluctance to grant this independence and their efforts to pry into the affairs of their children, their refusal to allow them a key, so that they know when they come in (and can ask where they have been), their failure to trust – all lead to constant friction.

Another important reason for friction is the fact that young people are beginning to think for themselves. Whereas, previously, a parent's word was accepted, there now has to be a good reason for a parental edict. Parents find that their past infallibility is now being questioned and they do not like it. They are not accustomed to having their word questioned. One frequent reply, 'Because I say so', does not go down well with a young person. When a young person, on being reprimanded, tries to explain his or her actions, many parents will snap back, 'Don't argue! Don't answer back!'

Young people can provoke friction at home in other ways. They may withdraw from the family circle into seclusion; they may direct scathing comments and sarcasm at their brothers and sisters; and they may be selfish. Also, choice of clothes, hairstyles and boy/girlfriends all lead to friction. When thwarted in their desires, some young people will call their parents 'horrible'.

Adults, too, have their personality problems. Much of the friction with children is due to their parents' intolerance, impatience and bad temper. Some teachers become angry with children who are slow to learn. Parents are impatient when children fail to understand instructions or forget what they have been told to do.

Another fault of parents is their failure to appreciate the sensitiveness of young people, who are readily offended by comments about their appearance, and by criticisms of their friends. Young people particularly resent being reprimanded in front of brothers and sisters. They hate to feel that derogatory remarks about them are being made behind their backs.

On the other hand parents feel thwarted because of their failure to stop various habits and forms of behaviour which they dislike in their adolescent children. When parents fail to stop young people making their rooms untidy, looking stupid in front of strangers because of shyness, or refusing to admit to a theft or breakage, there is bound to be deadlock.

Adapted from University of London Board
O-level English Language paper

How to Talk to your Mother

Reading aloud

In pairs, prepare a reading of the passage. You may wish to concentrate on three or four 'scenes' only. Try to adapt your use of volume, pace and stress to suit the particular mood and subject matter of each scene. Bear in mind that the passage is written in American English, but don't feel obliged to put on an accent!

Role-play

In pairs, make up one or two more scenes which could be added to the original passage. To do this, reread two or three of the original scenes to remind yourself of the tone and style of the original. Would you describe the series of arguments as:
– angry and confrontational?
– good-humoured, teasing and conciliatory?
– a mixture of these or neither of these?

Once you have agreed about the tone and style to use, decide on the identity of your two characters. Feel free to change 'daughter' to 'son' and 'mother' to 'father' if you wish. Then choose one or two of the following topics, or invent your own:

a You arrive home well after midnight to find the door locked. You have no key and so are obliged to ring the bell. You suspect that everybody has gone to bed.
b One of your parents disapproves of your current boy/girlfriend.
c You are being pressurised to do one of the following against your will: visit an ageing relative; go to a place of worship; attend one of your parents' favourite functions; accompany one or both of them to a parents' evening.

Write your scene either as a play script or in the same style as the original passage, then work out a reading of it either for taping or for acting out before the class.

Param-Jeet Runs Away from Home

Discussion and understanding

Read the passage at least twice, then discuss in a group or as a class the following questions:

a What appear to be the causes of the friction between Param-Jeet and his father (Babuji), which lead to the son's decision to run away?
b 'The only punishment, the only retributive measure he knew was the stick'. What light does this statement throw upon the way Babuji handles disputes with his son?
c Find three reasons why Sharan-Jeet did not want her brother to run away.

d What indications are there in the passage that Sharan-Jeet is not as highly regarded in the family as her brother? Why would this be?

e Do you believe that Param-Jeet acted in the right way? Could he have avoided friction with his father and yet kept to his plans of becoming an actor?

Creative writing

'The Home-coming'

In her autobiography, Sharan-Jeet describes how one of her uncles is dispatched to search for her brother in order to bring him back home. This uncle finds Param-Jeet, selling pens on a street corner in Bombay.

Draw on what you have learnt about the characters of Sharan-Jeet, Param-Jeet, Babuji and Mother, and write the story of the home-coming from the point of view of *one* of these four people. (For example, supposing you choose to be Param-Jeet, you might describe your feelings about the experience in Bombay, as well as your reactions to the moment of reunion with your parents.)

As in the original passage, include dialogue in your account to show the attitudes of each member of the family towards Param-Jeet's return.

Causes of Friction

Understanding and discussion

a Using only the information in 'Causes of Friction', identify and note down the reasons for friction between parents and young people saying whether it is:
- the fault of the young person
- the fault of the parent.

b Drawing on 'How To Talk To Your Mother', 'Causes of Friction' and your notes, discuss: *Is friction inevitable?*

Considering your own experiences where appropriate, discuss in groups or as a class the following issues:
- subjects which provoke grievances between you and your parents.
- subjects on which you and your parents generally tend to agree.
- responsibility for disputes: whose fault does it tend to be?
- do disputes have to happen or can they be avoided?
- ways of resolving disputes: how do *you* resolve them?
- are disputes necessarily a bad thing, or is there a case *for* them?

Discussion essay

'Friction between young people and their parents is inevitable.'

Give the arguments both for and against this statement, then justify your own view. Where appropriate, draw on your own experience to illustrate points made in your essay.

See *Techniques*: 'Drafting a discussion essay' for advice on drafting and writing this essay.

Drafting a discussion essay

Read this section to help you draft, edit and write a discussion essay.

A *discussion essay* puts forward two or more views of a subject. If this subject is a controversial one, you may be required to give the case both *for* and *against* it. Your own opinion is usually given at the end of the essay, based on the evidence you have presented.

An *argument essay* on the other hand, puts forward only one side of a controversial subject. Here your own opinion is very important because you are giving *your* views of an argument and attacking views which disagree with your own. (For advice on argument essays, see *Techniques*: 'Drafting an argument essay', chapter 8.)

If you are going to write a discussion essay, follow the advice given for this example:

'Friction between young people and their parents is inevitable.'

Give the case both for and against this view, then briefly justify your own view.

Stage 1   Content

1   Use any notes you have gathered from class discussion and study of the reading material to help you prepare your thoughts. Think carefully about what the essay title wants you to do.

2   Now prepare the points both for and against the view expressed in the essay title. To help you do this, divide a sheet of rough paper into two. In the *left*-hand column note down at least three main points *for* the view in the title, leaving several lines blank between each point. Do the same for the *right*-hand column, but this time, give points supporting the *opposing* view, in this way:

Friction is inevitable	Friction is avoidable .
1. Many young people need to assert their independence from their parents. This is bound to lead to friction because...	Asserting your own independence does not mean you have to be confrontational about it. There are alternative ways of behaving...

3 Now go back to each point and see whether you can develop it further. You can do this by:
  – explaining and giving reasons for each point;
  – illustrating a point by giving examples where appropriate, from your experience, from reading or perhaps from television.

4 Finally, jot down notes on your own view of the subject: that is, whether you agree or disagree with the view in the essay title. Alternatively, you may feel there is some truth in each side of the argument. Then note down the *reasons* for your own view.

Stage 2   Structure

You can now turn your list of points into a first draft. The structure of your essay (depending on length) should look something like this:

Paragraph 1/ Introduction :   Give an idea of what the essay is about, indicating how you intend to approach the subject matter.

Paragraph 2 :   Give your first point from the *left*-hand column of your rough notes – that is, defending the view in the essay title. Follow this with reasons and examples if appropriate.

Paragraph 3–4 :   Have a new paragraph for each new main point as above. Be sure that each new point is clearly indicated by a 'marker': e.g.' The third reason why parents often cause friction is . . .' (Note that if each of your points is quite short, you may have to group two or more points together in a single paragraph. If so, point 'markers' are essential.)'

Paragraphs 5–7 :   Give points from the *right*-hand column of your rough notes with reasons and examples.

Paragraph 8/ Conclusion :   Summarise what the essay has shown, giving your own view on the subject with reasons.

Stage 3   Editing

When you have written your first draft, examine it by asking yourself the questions below. When you feel that your essay satisfies the first question, go on to the next one. It may also be helpful to get a friend to read your work through as a check on any of the following:

1   Are the two sides of the discussion presented clearly and logically?

2   Does each paragraph indicate that it is making a new point, and where this point fits into the overall discussion?

3   Is your vocabulary accurate and appropriate? (Underline any words you feel could be improved. Find a better word by doing any of the following: consulting someone; using a Thesaurus; using a dictionary).

4   Have you checked your use of spelling, punctuation and grammar?

Stage 4   Writing

Now write the final version
of your discussion essay.

Facing up to the 'one-parent' family

All political parties claim to represent The Family – but what kind of family? One in three marriages today end in divorce and one in seven families are headed by a lone parent. Yet one parent families are still being penalised because of popular misconceptions about who they are. The family is changing, and the time has come to face up to the facts – rather than the fictions – of family life.

PREJUDICES

> *"One-parent families have enough problems without being saddled with myths"*
> **National Council for Voluntary Organisations**

"Lone parents are unmarried mothers"

Lone parents are of every age group, class, colour and nationality. The vast majority are people who have lost their partner through death or desertion. Only 16% are unmarried mothers, some of whom live with the child's father.

"One-parent families aren't proper families"

Two parents do not necessarily equal happiness for a family. Hence the growing number of divorces and separations. Nor does a failed marriage necessarily equal failed parenting. Most lone parents do a great job in difficult circumstances, and provide their children with love and emotional security.

> *"Clearly, life in single-parent families is often more difficult but no less caring"*
> **Home Office Report**

"Most delinquents come from broken homes"

There is no real evidence that children from one-parent families grow up any more disturbed or delinquent than their two parent counterparts. Most studies of child development show that apparent differences disappear once allowances are made for social class, poor housing, poverty and discrimination.

"Lone parents are scroungers"

Lone parents have little choice about their source of income. 48% are dependent on Supplementary Benefit. Many would prefer to go out to work, but cannot earn enough to pay childcare costs – if suitable childcare could be found.

Contrary to popular belief, maintenance is not a significant source of income for divorced women.

These commonly held prejudices go some way to explaining why one-parent families are considered – when they are considered at all – as a problem. But their main problem is that their needs are not being addressed.

PROBLEMS

One-parent families are not 'problem families' – but many of them are families with problems. Problems like:

POVERTY
48% of one-parent families have to claim Supplementary Benefit

HOUSING
Over half of Britain's homeless families are one-parent families

CHILDCARE
No government or local authority department has specific responsibility to provide out-of-school care for children, including those of working parents.

THE LEGAL SYSTEM
The adversarial nature of the legal system adds to the emotional upheaval of divorce and separation.

It is problems like these which undermine the security and well-being of one-parent families.

Ideally a whole range of measures is necessary to make major improvements for one-parent families. Measures like an expansion of the housing stock, full childcare provision and a guaranteed income. But we have to be realistic, and recognise the constraints under which all parties have to work.

Overleaf we propose some small reforms. They wouldn't transform the lives of lone parents and their children, but without costing a lot, they could improve them.

The Group Discussion (below) is not strictly part of the Case-study. It is included here so that you have a chance to study and discuss the issues raised by the reading material before starting the Case-study work.

Please also note that you can do the Case-study either as role-play, or as a real exercise. The NCOPF and Gingerbread welcome your letters and will read them, but may be unable to reply to you.

Group discussion

Read the Case-study material through at least twice, then discuss the following:

1 In your view what is the main message of the leaflet?

2 A number of 'prejudices' are mentioned in the leaflet.
   – What do you understand by this term as it is used here?
   – Find two separate words (or phrases) used in the leaflet's introduction which mean the same thing here as 'prejudice'.
   – Take each 'prejudice' in turn, starting with 'Lone Parents are Unmarried Mothers' and discuss the reasons why some people believe in each of these.

3 Discuss whether you agree with the claim by NCOPF and Gingerbread that the one-parent family can be as stable as the two-parent family, by answering these questions:
   – What are the advantages of the two-parent family?
   – What are the possible disadvantages?
   – What are the advantages of the one-parent family?
   – What are the possible disadvantages?

4 The NCOPF and Gingerbread suggest that the Government should offer one-parent families the same benefits as two-parent families and in some cases, extra benefits. For example, one of the campaign's policies (not mentioned in your reading material) is to persuade the Government 'to provide realistic out-of-school and holiday care for school-age children'. Look again at the 'Prejudices' and 'Problems' sections then discuss these questions:
   – Do you agree that one-parent families should be entitled to extra benefits such as childcare facilities?
   – If you do, what other benefits should there be?
   – Alternatively, do you feel that some discrimination against one-parent families is justified?
   – If you think so, try to explain why and say what form you think this should take.

'Facing Up To The (One-Parent) Family' was the name of a campaign run by the National Council for One Parent Families (NCOPF) and Gingerbread to make the general public more aware of the 'facts' about one-parent families in our society. Now the NCOPF and Gingerbread are interested to know the reactions of young people to some of their campaign publicity material and have sent samples of a leaflet to various schools and colleges including your own. They have invited individual students to write a letter to them, giving a frank response to the campaign leaflet. Choose *one* of the following three approaches.

1 Personal letter

Write a letter addressed to Gingerbread and the NCOPF, giving your own reaction to the information in the leaflet. Do this by drawing on the experience of a one-parent family you know, either to support some of the points in the leaflet or, indeed, to challenge them. Use the sections entitled 'Prejudices' and 'Problems' described in the leaflet to help you organise what you have to say. To do this, take one or more of the 'Prejudices' and comment on these from your own experience. Then move on to the 'Problems' and discuss whether any of these may apply to the family you describe.

   Go on to propose possible reforms the Government and society could make which would help the family to whom you have referred. If you feel that there are important points which the leaflet has failed to mention, raise them where appropriate.

2 Discussion letter

Write a letter to Gingerbread and the NCOPF, in which you take a more detached view of the issue of one-parent families than the 'personal letter' above. In your letter, discuss and give your opinion of what is being *said* in the leaflet – that is, its message – and particularly consider its significance for people of your age.

   You may wish to draw on some of the 'pointers' in the following letter plan to help you think through, and organise your comments:

Paragraph 1 : Your introduction
– State why you are writing the letter and what you intend to discuss.

Paragraph 2 : 'Prejudices' section
– What is the main message in this section and do you agree with it? Explain your view.
– In your experience, do young people share these 'prejudices' against one parent families?
– Do you feel that there are other 'prejudices' which the leaflet should mention?
– Do you think this section presents its message in a convincing way?

Paragraph 3 : 'Problems' section
– What is the main message in this section and do you agree with it? Explain your view.
– Are there any 'problems' not mentioned by the leaflet which ought to have been?
– What proposals for 'reforms' could you suggest to the NCOPF and Gingerbread which might help to counter some of the problems?

Paragraph 4 : Your conclusion
– In broad terms do you support or challenge the message in the leaflet?
– In brief, how would you like to see family life developing in the future?

3 Covering letter and leaflet

If you think that the leaflet could make its message more accessible to people of your age, then redesign all or part of it, using your own ideas. It may help you to follow this work plan:

a *Preparing your thoughts*
Note down what you like or dislike about the way the features below are presented in the leaflet:
Lay-out:
– the front (title) page
– the introduction and main sections
– the headings and sub-headings
– the information itself
– the different print sizes and colours
– the use of graphics and visuals (e.g. diagrams, illustrations, charts and so on).
Style of writing:
– the use of English: how clear and appropriate is the vocabulary and sentence structure for people of your age?
– the effect: is the writing sufficiently convincing?

b *Designing the leaflet*
Design draft lay-outs of the leaflet (or of chosen sections), which you include with your letter. You must use all the information provided but are free to present it differently. To do this, consider how you could use other ways of communicating such as diagrams, illustrations, charts and so on. (For general advice on designing a leaflet, see *Techniques*: 'Writing a Leaflet').
   (*Remember that the cost of producing these leaflets would prohibit the use of more than, say, two colours. The original leaflet has a yellow background, highlights some points on a background tint of grey, and uses a combination of black and white print.*)

c *The 'covering' letter*
Write a short 'covering' letter to the NCOPF and Gingerbread, giving a short explanation of your reasons for redesigning their campaign leaflet. Finish by suggesting what you hope to achieve by sending them your own version.

Writing a leaflet

Read this section to help you write a leaflet for the Case-study exercise on 'Facing Up To The (One-Parent) Family'.

A leaflet is a basic part of any publicity campaign and usually aims to persuade a mass audience to change its opinions and/or take a course of action, e.g. give a donation, become a member of an organisation. The style and contents of each leaflet will depend on who is going to read it and what it has to say. But it is possible to give you some general guidelines:

Title

The title of your leaflet should be eye-catching and informative. Well chosen puns and words with double meanings can be effective: e.g. *'Facing Up To* The Family'* implies both recognising a problem and having the courage to do something about it.

Structure

Your leaflet should be tightly organised into clear sections, with a logical sense of direction and purpose. It should be divided into the following sections:

a   *Introductory facts*: give the name of the campaigning group(s), the name and point of the campaign, the people at whom it is aimed.

b   *Main information sections*: first, give the reasons which make action necessary (e.g. 'Prejudices' and 'Problems'); second, offer the campaign's solutions ('Policies').

c   *Conclusion*: summarise the main argument and suggest what your readers can do to help the campaign. Perhaps finish with an eye-catching slogan!

The reader

Aim the text of your leaflet at a specific reader: e.g. If writing for young people of a particular age, express your points in a way that this group will understand without feeling patronised, and make your writing appeal to their interests and experience.

Content

Your leaflet should contain a mixture of hard facts, arguments and proposals. Each main point of an argument should be supported by hard facts (usually statistical evidence). Remember that you can only make a proposal if you have argued the case for it convincingly.

Style

Design your leaflet so that it can be read quickly. Points should be made as clearly, simply and concisely as possible without distorting the main argument. Avoid long chunks of text!

Presen-tation

Ensure that each heading and section is interesting to look at and easy to read. Variation can be introduced by using two or three colours; different print sizes; spacings; diagrams, charts and illustrations.

4

'LOVE
IS HEAVEN'

(Byron)

Page

A WEDDING IN VIEW
Lonely Hearts

Can someone make my simple wish come true?
Male biker seeks female for touring fun.
Do you live in North London? Is it you?

Gay vegetarian whose friends are few,
I'm into music, Shakespeare and the sun.
Can someone make my simple wish come true?

Executive in search of something new −
Perhaps bisexual woman, arty, young.
Do you live in North London? Is it you?

Successful, straight and solvent? I am too −
Attractive Jewish lady with a son.
Can someone make my simple wish come true?

I'm Libran, inexperienced and blue −
Need slim non-smoker, under twenty-one.
Do you live in North London? Is it you?

Please write (with photo) to Box 152.
Who knows where it may lead once we've begun?
Can someone make my simple wish come true?
Do you live in North London? Is it you?

Wendy Cope

Stags and Hens

The following play extract is set in a Liverpool dance hall. It is here that Dave and Linda have each decided, without the other one's knowledge to hold their stag and hen parties. In this scene, Linda and her three friends, Bernadette, Frances and Carol are in the 'Ladies', getting themselves ready for the dance floor...

LINDA	Why don't y' all come on me honeymoon?
BERNADETTE	We would Linda love, but I'm afraid if I was there, you wouldn't get a look in.
	The GIRLS, *apart from* LINDA, *laugh.*
LINDA	Look ... I am a big girl now y'know. I can find me way out of the Ladies an' into the dance.
BERNADETTE	Linda ... it's your hen night, we stick with you.
LINDA	Yeh, until some feller wants t' take you outside. Then you'll be off like a flash.
BERNADETTE	Well ... you've got to get a bit of fresh air haven't you?
LINDA	Is that what you call it?
BERNADETTE	With some of them that's what it feels like!
	Shrieks from the GIRLS.
LINDA	Well you'd better watch out tonight, Berni. You're gonna have a bit of competition.
BERNADETTE	Ooh. Tch. Who from?
LINDA	Well y'don't think I'm gonna end my hen night stuck in the bar like some old married woman do y'? I'm gonna get out on that floor an' forget about everythin' else. I'm gonna get real legless. If it's a last fling then that's what I'm gonna make it.
FRANCES	Well y' better get a move on or your last fling'll be already flung. Come here, let me do it. Go on, you lot go ... y' can be gettin' the drinks in.
CAROL	Yeh ... come on then ... what y' havin'?
FRANCES	Get us a port an' lemon. What d'y' want, Linda?
LINDA	Get me a pint of bitter.
BERNADETTE	Linda love, no come on. A joke's a joke. I've seen you do that before love and we all think it's a good laugh. But not tonight. It's a hen night you're on, not a stag night. Now come on, something a bit more lady-like.
LINDA	All right, I'll have a pint of mild!
BERNADETTE	Oh sod off ...
CAROL	We'll get y' a Snowball Linda, y'like them.
LINDA	All right. With a nice little cherry on the top.
BERNADETTE	Come on. We'll be in the bar.
CAROL	We'll just have a drink an' listen to the sounds till you come out...
BERNADETTE	Ogh ... come on. Give us some music. Music, music, music. It's an aphrodisiac to me.
LINDA	Bromide'd be an aphrodisiac to you.
BERNADETTE	Too right ... ooogh ... come on girls...
	They go into the corridor and exit.
	FRANCES *is fixing* LINDA's *hair and make-up.*

FRANCES	It's great the way the music gets to y' though, isn't it? Y' can come to a disco or a dance an' be feelin' really last. But once y' walk into the music it gives y' a lift doesn't it? Makes y' feel special.
LINDA	Yeh. (*After a pause.*) I get lost in music I do.
FRANCES	Yeh I do that.
LINDA	I become someone else when the music's playin'. I do y' know.
FRANCES	Yeh I'm like that.
LINDA	D' y' know if it wasn't for music I wouldn't be gettin' married tomorrow.
FRANCES	(*laughing*) Oh don't be stupid Linda. You're nuts sometimes. Y' are y' know.
LINDA	I'm not bein' stupid. We were dancin' when he asked me to marry him. 'When A Man Loves A Woman' it was. I heard this voice in me ear, like it was part of the music, sayin' 'Will y' marry me?' So I said yeh. I would've said yeh if I'd been dancin' with Dracula's ugly brother.
FRANCES	Linda stop bein' soft.
LINDA	When the music stopped I looked up an' there was Dave, beamin' down at me, talkin' about gettin' married an' I'm wonderin' what he's on about, then I remembered. An' the next thing y' know I'm here tonight.
FRANCES	Linda!
LINDA	Oh come on, hurry up an' get me hair done. All I wanna do is get out there an' dance the night away. There mightn't be another opportunity after tonight.
FRANCES	Linda, you're gettin' married, not gettin' locked up! There y' go. (*She begins putting her implements away.*)
LINDA	(*looking at herself in the mirror*) Y' do get frightened y' know. I mean if it was just gettin' married to Dave it'd be OK, he's all right Dave is. But it's like, honest, it's like I'm gettin' married to a town.
FRANCES	To a what?
LINDA	It's not just like I'm marryin' Dave. It's like if I marry him I marry everythin'. Like, I could sit down now an' draw you a chart of everythin' that'll happen in my life after tomorrow.
FRANCES	(*looking at her*) D' y' know something Linda, you're my best mate, but half the time I think you're a looney!
LINDA	(*going into an exaggerated looney routine*) I am ... (*She plays it up.*)
FRANCES	(*laughing*) Linda ... don't mess y' hair up ...
LINDA	(*quickly knocking her hair back into place, preparing to leave*) Well ... look at it this way, after tomorrow I'll have me own Hoover, me own colour telly an' enough equipment to set up a chain of coffee bars.

They go into the corridor and exit.

Willy Russell

Portrait of the Artist as a Young Dog

This passage is from one of Dylan Thomas' memoirs of growing up in South Wales in the 1920s. The memoir recounts how he goes on a camping holiday with three friends, Sidney, Dan and George. Near the beach they meet Brazell and Skully, 'the worst and biggest boys in school', who follow them down to the sea and tease George, the smallest in the group. As this is going on, three girls appear.

Three girls, all fair, came down the cliff-side arm in arm, dressed in short, white trousers. Their arms and legs and throats were brown as berries; I could see when they laughed that their teeth were very white; they stepped on to the beach, and Brazell and Skully stopped singing. Sidney smoothed his hair back, rose casually, put his hands in his pockets, and walked towards the girls, who now stood close together, gold and brown, admiring the sunset with little attention, patting their scarves, turning smiles on each other. He stood in front of them, grinned, and saluted: 'Hallo, Gwyneth! do you remember me?'

'La-di-da!' whispered Dan at my side, and made a mock salute to George still peering at the retreating sea.

'Well, if this isn't a surprise!' said the tallest girl. With little studied movements of her hands, as though she were distributing flowers, she introduced Peggy and Jean.

Fat Peggy, I thought, too jolly for me, with hockey legs and tomboy crop, was the girl for Dan: Sidney's Gwyneth was a distinguished piece and quite sixteen, as immaculate and unapproachable as a girl in Ben Evans' stores; but Jean, shy and curly, with butter-coloured hair, was mine. Dan and I walked slowly to the girls.

I made up two remarks: 'Fair's fair, Sidney, no bigamy abroad,' and 'Sorry we couldn't arrange to have the sea in when you came.'

Jean smiled, wriggling her heel in the sand, and I raised my cap.

'Hallo!'

The cap dropped at her feet.

As I bent down, three lumps of sugar fell from my blazer pocket. 'I've been feeding a horse,' I said, and began to blush guiltily when all the girls laughed.

I could have swept the ground with my cap, kissed my hand gaily, called them señoritas, and made them smile without tolerance. Or I could have stayed at a distance, and this would have been better still, my hair blown in the wind, though there was no wind at all that evening, wrapped in mystery and staring at the sun, too aloof to speak to girls; but I knew that all the time my ears would have been burning, my stomach would have been as hollow and as full of voices as a shell. 'Speak to them quickly, before they go away!' a voice would have said insistently over the dramatic silence, as I stood like Valentino on the edge of the bright, invisible bull-ring of the sands. 'Isn't it lovely here!' I said.

I spoke to Jean alone; and this is love, I thought, as she nodded her head and swung her curls and said: 'It's nicer than Porthcawl.'

Brazell and Skully were two big bullies in a nightmare; I forgot them when Jean and I walked up the cliff, and, looking back to see if they were baiting George again or wrestling together, I saw that George had disappeared around the corner of the rocks and that they were talking at the foot of the cliff with Sidney and the two girls.

'What's your name?'

I told her.

'That's Welsh,' she said.

'You've got a beautiful name.'

'Oh, it's just ordinary.'

'Shall I see you again?'

'If you want to.'

'I want to all right! We can go and bathe in the morning. And we can try to get an eagle's egg. Did you know that there were eagles here?'

'No,' she said. 'Who was that handsome boy on the beach, the tall one with dirty trousers?'

'He's not handsome, that's Brazell. He never washes or combs his hair or anything. He's a bully and he cheats.'

'I think he's handsome.'

We walked into Button's field, and I showed her inside the tents and gave her one of George's apples. 'I'd like a cigarette,' she said.

It was nearly dark when the others came. Brazell and Skully were with Gwyneth, one each side of her holding her arms, Sidney was with Peggy, and Dan walked, whistling, behind with his hands in his pockets.

'There's a pair,' said Brazell, 'they've been here all alone and they aren't even holding hands. You want a pill,' he said to me.

'Build Britain's babies,' said Skully.

'Go on!' Gwyneth said. She pushed him away from her, but she was laughing, and she said nothing when he put his arm around her waist.

'What about a bit of fire?' said Brazell.

Jean clapped her hands like an actress. Although I knew I loved her, I didn't like anything she said or did.

'Who's going to make it?'

'He's the best, I'm sure,' she said, pointing at me.

Dan and I collected sticks, and by the time it was quite dark there was a fire crackling. Inside the sleeping-tent, Brazell and Jean sat close together; her golden head was on his shoulder; Skully, near them, whispered to Gwyneth; Sidney unhappily held Peggy's hand.

'Did you ever see such a sloppy lot?' I said, watching Jean smile in the fiery dark.

'Kiss me, Charley!' said Dan.

We sat by the fire in the corner of the field. The sea, far out, was still making a noise. We heard a few nightbirds. '"Tu-whit! tu-whoo!" Listen! I don't like owls,' Dan said, 'they scratch your eyes out!' – and tried not to listen to the soft voices in the tent. Gwyneth's laughter floated out over the suddenly moonlit field, but Jean, with the beast, was smiling and silent in the covered warmth; I knew her little hand was in Brazell's hand.

'Women!' I said.

Dan spat in the fire.

Dylan Thomas

The Scarlet Thread

In this chapter from her autobiography, Sita Devi, an Indian woman now living in Britain, describes the Hindu wedding ceremony of her sister, Indira. The wedding is typical of those held within the Hindu tradition of arranged marriages.

One of my earliest memories is of the wedding of Indira, my second sister. The first was married before I can remember. How old I was then I do not know. We had no birth certificates or any other records to tell us, so people would remember a birth or a death by some special happening at the same time. I asked once when I was born and was told it was well remembered because everyone was so disappointed . . . I was the fifth girl in the family. My mother began to worry as soon as I was born about how she would find the money to marry me off! This was always the way in the village; to be unmarried was unthinkable. A woman without a husband was not a person at all. And this is how even a widow is considered. For the rest of her life after the death of her husband she is a person of no importance; she must dress simply in white or very pale colours, wear no jewellery or make-up, and of course she will usually be poor without a man to support her. If she has children she is of more account, and her relatives will probably help her more, but as a woman she is supposed to be finished, even if still young. Her relatives may try to find a man to marry her, and if they do, the ceremony is very small, with no rejoicing. Even in death the widow is not honoured as others are, and has a very simple funeral. You can see from this how important it is for girls to get married; it is looked upon as the most important thing in their lives.

Unless they are wealthy, the parents must sacrifice themselves for their daughters, providing them with dowries and paying for the wedding feast. It is also a great responsibility for them as their daughter's happiness and well-being depend on the parents being able to make a good choice. All village marriages are arranged and much bargaining takes place. Everything must be weighed up carefully. Are the young people of the right caste, are they matched in education, in their families' wealth and respectability, in looks and health, in personality and ability? Opinions are asked for all around, and secret investigations made, for who knows if the other side is telling the truth? Of course however careful the parents are there is still a lot of luck in it, for whether marriages are arranged or left to choice, as in this country, there is no way of being certain how it will turn out.

Once parents have agreed, the wedding preparations can start. It becomes a time of excitement, hope and happiness, even if it is a great worry to the family concerned. They know that they will in turn be able to enjoy the many weddings of their relatives and friends, all through their lives, and this makes the effort even more worthwile. A month before the wedding, relatives and friends come around to help. A tailor is employed to make new clothes for all the family and for the in-laws too. The bride must have a beautiful wedding sari in bright red and gold, and many more to take away with her. Even a poor girl should have ten at least, and a rich girl might have a hundred, some made of silk and embroidered by hand. There is a goldsmith in the village and the bride visits him to choose her jewellery, as she must have some gold for her wedding. This gold, though, is not pure, and like our silver has other metal in it, so it is not as expensive as purer gold would be. She can ask for special designs to her own taste, and is expected to have a necklace and earrings at the very least. If she comes of a rich family she will also have rings, bangles, anklets, nose jewellery, and ornaments for the hair and the hands, some set with precious stones. Meanwhile, preparations for the feasts and parties are going on, and these are considerable – as, for instance, when Indira was married we had two hundred guests, some from the groom's side, some from ours. Many came from distant villages and had to be put up for two nights at least, and fed too, very generously. It was no wonder Mother had to go to the village moneylender and pay back for so many years.

A week before the wedding relatives and friends of the bride come every day to dance and sing and play instruments in her home. She cannot join in, but she can enjoy all the excitement and anticipation. She has never before had such rich and beautiful saris and jewels, make-up and perfume to wear, nor has she ever been so important. Of course she must wonder about her husband, especially if he comes from a distant village and she does not know him, even by sight. And of course she learns all she can about him from her family and friends, and hopes she will fall in love as soon as she sees him. Then three days before the wedding there is a special custom, the same for the bride and groom, but kept separate. Friends and relatives come to their houses bringing rice which is boiled and eaten with milk and sugar or with brown lentils, to bring good luck. Then bride and groom are bathed and their faces and limbs are rubbed with 'manya', a preparation of oil and turmeric and other spices to make their skin smooth and beautiful.

The night before the wedding, they see each other for the first time, though only for a moment. The groom comes to the bride's door and she will have made herself as pretty as she can, putting on one of her new saris and doing her hair in a becoming style. She opens the door to him and he brings a garland of gold and silver flowers to place round her neck. She has another garland of gold and silver flowers for him. This is very romantic, especially if they like the look of each other.

Our guests were to sleep on mats on the floor in the house and his were to have the village hall. I remember we borrowed a quilt, pillow and sheet for each guest from our neighbours, and these were lent willingly as it is everyone's duty to help with a wedding. The bridegroom's family must also do some preparation. The groom must have new clothes; if he is rich these may be very splendid, but if he is poor he must at least have a good suit, a gold ring and a watch. He must bring a few especially fine saris for his bride and some expensive jewellery. When he comes to the wedding he should ride in a car decorated with flowers, or on a horse also decorated. His family comes too and they are accompanied by musicians and dancers who will play and sing and amuse the company for perhaps several days. You can see that everything is done to make our weddings beautiful and full of colour and romance. Everyone rejoices, and even if life is hard afterwards there is something wonderful to remember. I always thought I should have a wedding like this, and like most girls I used to dream about it and picture it in my mind. All these years later I sometimes imagine myself in such a dream, as my own wedding was so different.

You may be surprised to hear that our wedding ceremony takes place at three o'clock in the morning, so no one gets any sleep that night. The last preparations for the feast will be made at this time. The house will be made ready for the priest who will be coming to celebrate the wedding, and for all the guests. In the centre of the main room a special fire is lit; the wood for this is scented and sprinkled with ghee, which is clarified butter. Bride and groom stand close together so that her sari can be tied to his waist sash, signifying that they are now united. Then, with him leading, they circle around the

fire seven times while the priest says prayers, stopping briefly after each circle is made. These prayers are in Sanscrit, which only the Brahmins know, so I have never understood what is said. When this is finished the man and the woman are a married couple, but they do not kiss each other as people do here. Bride and groom then separate and walk around the village or by the canals with their guests, and everyone wishes to see them and talk to them.

– ☆ –

Next day the guests must be fed again, and in some cases they may stay for a week or more. And there are two more little rites for bride and groom after the wedding. Each has a scarlet thread, knotted many times, made into a bracelet and put on the wrist, and she must undo his and he hers. The knots are very tight and hard to untie, and if they do not know each other and feel shy it makes them used to touching each other and sharing a task. It is meant to remind them that there are many knotty problems to come in married life which they should help each other to overcome. Then a tub of water is brought in and they sit beside it. A woman throws in a coin and they must compete to get it first. They are bound to laugh and struggle to win and this breaks the tension between them. This is done several times, and it is said that the one who wins will be the one to rule, but sometimes if the girl wins she will give the coin to her husband to save his pride and show she does not want to be the boss!

At last husband and wife are alone together. She is supposed to lose her virginity the first night, and their sheet should be stained with blood. This can be seen by the relatives next day, and if it cannot, whatever the cause, the girl will be disgraced and despised by her husband and both families, and everyone in the village will soon know. When I came to this country I learned that some innocent girls do not have intact hymens, so they suffer for nothing, but this is not generally accepted by Indians. I think we are certainly very ignorant about sex; I know I was when my turn to get married came. We would never have dared to ask our mothers to tell us, and even sisters and close friends never spoke about it. My eldest brother was different. I know this as I went to his wedding in Delhi and travelled back home with him and Sadesh in the train. All through the night he was talking to her very gently and getting to know her. Educated men like Krishna would not force themselves on their brides.

told by Sita Devi.
written down by Rachel Barton.

The reading material on the previous pages reveals various perspectives on sex, love and marriage. The discussion activity below asks you to consider some commonly stated views on the subject:

Discussion

In small groups choose *one* of the commonplace statements below to discuss further. As a group, find at least three reasons supporting the view expressed in the statement and three or more reasons opposing this view. Then try to come to a consensus – that is a group agreement about whether you all support the statement or not.

- 'People who resort to advertising in "Lonely Hearts" columns or using marriage bureaux must be desperate.'

- 'Marrying for love does not guarantee a successful marriage.'

- 'There is too much pressure in our society to get married. With our high divorce rate, it would be better if more people stayed single.'

- 'Whatever your cultural background, parents should still have a say in your choice of marriage partner.'

Lonely
Hearts

Creative writing

After reading the poem and the 'Lonely Hearts' adverts at the beginning of the chapter, see if you can write some poetry of your own on the same theme. Perhaps choose one of these two approaches:

1 *Advertisement poem*: write a five-line poem drawing on the content of one of the 'Lonely Hearts' adverts. The first and last lines simply name the person who is advertising. The middle three or four lines describe this person in more detail and give an idea of the partner they are looking for. Where possible, use your imagination to develop the portrait of the 'lonely heart'. As each word in an advertisement costs money, make sure that its sound and meaning both help to convey the person's character. For example:

Executive, 52,	*Jewish lady,*
Short, plump, rich,	*Stunning, dark-eyed jewel,*
In search of something new,	*A wealthy widow with career,*
A bisexual girl who's into Art?	*And son away at school,*
Executive, 52.	*Wants solvent man for adventure,*
	Jewish lady.

2 *In the manner of Wendy Cope*: try using the same verse structure as the poem 'Lonely Hearts', keeping the wording in upright print the same

as the original, but substituting the italic print with your own ideas. Perhaps rewrite the poem using the bordering adverts as your source material. So, for example, the 'Peter Pan' advert might become the subject of your first 'stanza' (verse), and the 'Manchester Man' your second.

Discussion

Ask for volunteers from the class to read the play extract aloud, then discuss these questions in small groups:

1 What are the signs that Linda may be experiencing last-minute nerves about her marriage to Dave? Trace these signs through the scene.

2 What do you learn of the relationship between Linda and Dave?

3 Explain Linda's fears for her future with Dave. What does marriage appear to mean to her?

4 What are the 'fors' and 'againsts' of meeting someone at a dance or disco? Is a point of view indicated in this scene?

5 'Stag' and 'hen' parties are part of the social ritual of many Western weddings. Do you believe they have a value? What other rituals are part of Western weddings? Which of these rituals still have a value today? Which are outdated in your view?

Creative writing

Choose *one* of the subjects below and write a play script for it. If possible, either use a Liverpudlian style of speech as in the scene, or if you prefer, use the style of speech from your own region. When you have completed your script, read each other's scripts in groups. Perhaps choose one of these to read/act out, before the class.

1 Write an equivalent scene set in the Gents involving Dave and his three friends, Billy, Kav and Eddy. In this, Dave expresses his intentions for the evening, his feelings about the wedding the next day and his views on marrying Linda.

2 Write a scene much later on in the evening when things have happened which Dave and Linda may regret. Choose *one* of the following incidents:
   – In the Ladies again: Linda has embarrassed her friends.
   – In the Gents: one of Dave's friends has spotted Linda having 'a final fling'. What do they do?
   – Linda and Dave meet unexpectedly on the dance floor.

Discussion and understanding

1   How does Thomas suggest the physical attraction between the boys and the girls when they first meet? To answer this, study the *first* paragraph and select words or phrases which indicate this.

2   Consider Thomas' thoughts about approaching the three girls in the paragraph beginning, 'I could have swept the ground . . .' What expectations does he have of how he should behave with girls?

3   Look at Jean's behaviour through the passage. What does she say or do which suggests that she is rather different from Thomas' first impression of her?

4   What clues are given *before* the fire is made that Brazell is to be a threat to Thomas' friendship with Jean?

5   Why do you think Thomas fails to 'win' Jean? Look at the way he behaves with Jean during the passage.

6   Why do you think Thomas' prediction of which girl would be suitable for which boy, turns out to be so wrong?

7   Read carefully the paragraph beginning, 'We sat by the fire . . .' How does this indicate the way Thomas is feeling?

Creative writing

Choose *one* of the following:

1   Retell the story in the pasage as if you are one of the three girls. Try to give your first impressions of the boys, your hopes for the day and whether these are fulfilled by what happens.

2   Imagine you are either Brazell or Sidney. Retell the story from his point of view, indicating how you feel about what happens to you.

3   Imagine you are either Thomas or Jean. You meet unexpectedly on the beach the day after the camp fire. Write about how you meet, what you say to each other and how you part. Show how events may have changed the first impression you had of each other.

Discussion and understanding

Read the passage through carefully, preferably twice. Use the following questions either as a basis for discussion and/or for written answers:

1 From your reading of the passage, what do you understand by the term 'arranged marriage'?

2 Why is it considered so important for Hindu girls, particularly in the villages of India, to be married?

3 The passage shows that there are various stages to an Indian wedding, from the preparations to the wedding night. Chart each stage, noting down the main activities associated with it.
   e.g. A month before: early preparations – tailor makes new clothes for the family, bride and in-laws, and so on.

4 If you are familiar with the pattern of weddings from Western or any other culture, chart its stages in the way you have just done for the Hindu wedding.
   Which features are similar in the weddings from the two cultures? Which are different?

5 Weddings from all cultures involve 'rites'. What do you understand by this word? How does a 'rite' differ from a 'ritual'?
   What do you think may be the significance of the following rites performed by the couple during a Hindu wedding?
   – the exchange of garlands;
   – circling a fire seven times as the priest says prayers;
   – undoing each other's scarlet threaded bracelet;
   – the competition to rescue coins from a tub.

Writing

Choose one of the following topics:

1 Describe a Western wedding or one from another culture, as if you were explaining it to Hindu people in India. Imagine your description is to appear as an article in an English-speaking magazine in India.

2 Retell the story in the passage through the eyes of Indira or her husband-to-be. Try to convey your person's hopes and fears before the wedding, the first impressions of their marriage partner and the emotions experienced when they first meet alone.

3 Write a discussion essay using *one* of the statements in the Discussion exercise on p. 00 as your basis. (For a discussion essay see *Techniques*: 'Drafting a discussion essay', chapter 3.)

COMPUTER DATING

Dateline

'She was too attractive!'

Dateline

'My life was pretty boring,' confessed Tim. 'My two best friends moved away — one to Germany and the other to university — and I never really went out. One night I was listening to Radio Luxembourg when I heard the Dateline advert and I thought I might as well join.'

Tim Smith has always lived in Wells-Next-The-Sea in Norfolk. Wells being quite literally 'next the sea', it's maybe not surprising that 22 year old Tim is an in-shore fisherman. It's a job he enjoys, but it didn't do anything for his social life.

Tim sent off for the Dateline details but it took him a couple of months to pluck up the courage to actually join. But join he did and soon got his first list of four names.

'I met one girl from Norwich, but she wasn't really my type,' he said. Not daunted, he was preparing to send off for another computer run when a letter dropped through his letter box. An ordinary enough occurrence, but one which was to change his life, because the letter was from Suzanne Anderson, who had got his name and address from Dateline.

Suzanne, an attractive 19 year old assembly line worker from Kings Lynn, joined Dateline because she wanted to find one special boyfriend. 'I was a bit fed up. I had just finished some amateur dramatics and I had nothing else to do.' Unlike Tim, she didn't hesitate and joined Dateline as soon as she received the details. Tim was the first person she contacted. 'I sent him my phone number on the Friday and he phoned me two days later,' said Sue.

'We were both nervous,' remembered Tim, 'but she seemed friendly.' Fortunately Sue felt the same about Tim and the couple decided to meet outside the Conservative Club in Kings Lynn. Sue sent Tim a photograph of herself so he was able to recognise her when he arrived. He was very impressed with what he saw as he drove up. 'I thought she was too attractive to be a member of Dateline,' said Tim, laughing. 'I thought they would all be ugly.'

Sue and Tim went for a drink in the town centre and got on so well together that they went on for a steak together at the local 'Bernie', the Globe. Afterwards Tim took Sue home where they talked until one o'clock in the morning! 'It was as though we had known each other for years,' said Tim. Sue was delighted when Tim asked to see her again although 'I didn't expect him to, really,' she said, and the couple met two nights later. 'We went out virtually every night after that and it felt as though we had known each other for years. It was amazing really,' said Sue.

Nine days after they first met, Tim asked Sue to get engaged and she said yes. 'I was quite surprised,' she said. 'I didn't think he would ask me that quickly, although I was secretly hoping he would.'

The speed with which Sue and Tim found each other has surprised their friends and relatives — Suzanne was only on the Dateline computer for three weeks! 'Some people thought it was a little bit soon, but they're getting over the shock now,' said Sue. 'They all like Tim.'

Tim's family have also got over their surprise and the wedding is planned for two years' time — plenty of opportunity for Sue and Tim to develop their relationship. In the meantime, Tim is in no doubt about the improvement in his lifestyle, thanks to Dateline. 'I would tell anyone to join Dateline,' he said. 'It will improve their social life no end. Before, I was sitting at home all the time and now I am never there! I have been out every night now for a month and I have been to places where I have never been before.'

And how does he feel about computer dating now?

'Before I joined Dateline I thought that the only people who used dating agencies were the real

lonely-hearts types — that they were all ugly — but they're just normal people, very friendly.'

'Yes,' said Sue, 'I had a similar picture of Dateline. I was really surprised and I would definitely encourage people to join. They should have a go and see what happens.'

Just like Tim and Sue did…!

Profile of John Goodier

Factual brief

24-year-old production worker.

Reasons for joining Dateline: His work didn't bring him into contact with girls. Met several girls but weren't his type. Had just received his second list of names.

First meeting: Had a brief description of Veronica but didn't fit this to the girl outside Lewis's; waited until *she* introduced herself. Seemed to have a lot in common; very much wanted to see her again.

Relationship: Continued to make arrangements to see Veronica; very taken by her; knew that she was special after only three weeks, that he was in love with her at the Christmas party. Planned a holiday with her, then saw how this might fit into marriage plans: proposed in January.

   John's parents 'delighted' with the news: had already welcomed Veronica into the family.

   Although apprehensive about joining *Dateline* at first, now recommends it to anyone who wishes to improve their social life.

John Goodier's comments
(from Press Office interview)

'I'm in the middle of my tea. Can you ring me back in 15 minutes please?' (*John's first ever sentence to Veronica*.)

'I had a brief description, but we hadn't exchanged descriptions so I was standing there and I saw this coloured girl standing close by. I thought, "She's really nice looking." I wondered if this was her?'

'She nearly collapsed in my arms.'

'We were absolutely perfect. She's just right for me. She's got such a great personality and we get on so well together. I have just never met a girl like her before.'

'There's no point hanging around any longer, I'll ask her.'

'How about postponing the holiday? How about getting engaged first and then going on holiday?' (*John's proposal to Veronica*.)

'It's made my life a whole lot better.'

Profile of Veronica Bobb

Factual brief

21-year-old office worker.

Reasons for joining Dateline: She was unhappy with her social life: for instance, there was no one to accompany her to the Christmas party at work.

John Goodier the first name on the list *Dateline* sent to her. Decided to ring him rather than write. Although an unnerving experience for her, they chatted for nearly an hour; arranged to meet outside Lewis's in Manchester, the following week.

First meeting: Three men standing outside Lewis's all fitted John's description – two left and she was able to approach John. Went for a pizza and got on very well; arranged to meet again.

Relationship: At first she was tentative; met other people from the *Dateline* list, but none she liked as much as John. Met regularly; particularly enjoyed her Christmas with him, but was stunned when he proposed unexpectedly in January. Had not realised how strong her feelings were and accepted.

Worried about telling her parents about the engagement, but they were delighted. Still hasn't plucked up courage to tell them *how* she met John.

Commends *Dateline* as a way of meeting people – better than being 'picked up'.

Veronica Bobb's comments
(from Press Office interview)

'I have been out with a few men and I was involved in a relationship for about three or four months. I was getting a bit serious but the man wasn't, so that ended.'

'I'm not a shy person, but it is usually the norm that the man gets in touch with the girl so it seemed really brazen to me, but there was no other way I could have made contact, apart from writing.'

'I have a passion for cartoons, especially "He Man" and John was writing for "He Man" magazine. Then I found out he actually collects cartoons – I was speechless!'

'John had blue eyes, but there was no way I was going close up to fellows to see if they had blue eyes! They were all fair and over six foot.'

'It was not anything to do with colour, but my Mum and Dad don't believe in whirlwind relationships – you have got to see someone for seven years then start holding hands.'

'I cannot imagine life without John now. I have never felt this way about a man before. I have met a whole new lot of people.'

You have recently started your first job as a trainee assistant to the Press Officer at *Dateline*, the well-known computer dating service. As part of your training, your first main assignment is to design and write some publicity material featuring a young couple, who represent a special success for *Dateline*. The computer service has always featured white, European couples in its publicity. This is mainly because less than 10% of *Dateline* members are from other racial backgrounds and the 'success stories' amongst this group have been unwilling so far to be featured. However, a young couple, Veronica Bobb (black), and John Goodier (white), who met through *Dateline* and are engaged to be married, have agreed to be used for publicity. As you are a trainee, you have been told that your design work and writing will be considered seriously, but not necessarily used.

   You have been given a number of resource materials from which you are expected to draw all your information, and to get ideas. These are:
– a profile of Veronica Bobb and of John Goodier based on an interview carried out by your Press Office;
– an article featuring another young couple, which you have been asked to use as a model for your own article;
– a standard extract from *Dateline* adverts summarising the value of its service.

1 Poster

Design the rough lay-out and text for a poster, to be placed in public places where people are generally on the move – such as on an escalator wall in the London Underground. You have been advised that the poster should:
– remind the public of *Dateline*'s name and service;
– communicate its message at a glance.

2 Newspaper article

Write an article featuring the success story of how Veronica Bobb and John Goodier met through *Dateline* and soon got engaged to be married. The article is to be used mainly in *Dateline*'s own newspaper, 'Dateline News', circulated to its members. But also, it may be featured in magazine adverts encouraging other single people to join *Dateline*.

   In drafting your article, use the profiles of Veronica and John on pp. 72–3, and draw on the approach of the sample article, 'She was too attractive!' Remember that you may only use the information supplied, but can choose to emphasise certain points and if necessary leave out others. You have been told that the article should:
– advertise the successful service *Dateline* operates;
– stress *Dateline*'s role as a service for young, single, ordinary people who may be missing out on a good social life.

3 Radio commercial

Write the script for a 30-second radio commercial for your local radio station advertising the service *Dateline* offers and featuring Veronica and John. You have been told that the advert is aiming to:
– get across *Dateline*'s credentials simply and attractively;
– appeal to young, single people looking for a better social life.

(Use the *Techniques* advice below to help you write a radio script.)

Writing a script for a radio commercial

A script for a radio commercial may combine any of the following elements:

Commentary : a 'voice over' narrating or explaining the subject matter – either by a professional broadcaster, or by someone involved in the commercial.

Dialogue : spoken by two or more of the people involved, usually a conversation.

Sound effects : any sounds other than speech used to create a sense of 'background' such as music, footsteps, traffic, birdsong, and so on.

A typical layout for a script should look like this.

Subject: *Title*:

	Time	Sound effects	Commentary/dialogue

Narrating

Narrating is a style of speaking or writing when:
– you are telling a story;
– you are recalling what has happened to you or to other people.

You will find the narrating style in many types of writing including stories, (auto)biography, diaries, newspaper articles, jokes, anecdotes and songs.
    It has at least three main features:
– order of events
– past or present?
– viewpoint.

1 Order of events

When you narrate, you tell the reader about a number of events in a certain order.
    In the *Dateline* advertisement in this chapter, the story of how Tim and Sue met is told in the order in which it happened:

You can tell the same story in a different order, which will change its emphasis and perhaps its meaning:

a Which of the two versions is the more effective and why?
    (Remember that the story is an advert for *Dateline*.)
b Which version would be the more effective if you were rewriting the *Dateline* advert as a magazine love story?

2 Past or present?

When you narrate, you either tell what is happening in the present, or you tell what has happened in the past.

Most writers prefer to use the past tense when they narrate. After all, they are usually looking back on something that has already happened. Compare the effect of this passage from the *Dateline* article when written in the past and then in the present tense:

> 'Sue and Tim went for a drink in the town centre and got on so well together that they went for a steak together at the local *Berni*, the "Globe".'
>
> 'Sue and Tim go for a drink in the town centre and get on so well together that they go for a steak together at the local *Berni*, the "Globe".'

a How do you think the use of the present tense alters the sense here?

b Can you think of instances in speech or writing when you might use the present tense to tell a story?

3 Viewpoint

When you tell a story or recall an event, you have to decide on the narrator's viewpoint. Are you involved personally in the action? Or are you standing outside the action?

If you are involved personally, you will narrate in the first person ('I'). But if you are narrating as someone outside the action, you will use the third person (he/she). Compare the viewpoints used in the following two passages:

> 'Our guests were to sleep on the floor in the house and his were to have the village hall. I remember we borrowed a quilt, pillow and sheet for each guest from our neighbours and these were lent willingly as it is everyone's duty to help with a wedding.'
>
> *The Scarlet Thread*
>
> '. . . he [Tim] was preparing to send off for another computer run when a letter dropped through his letterbox. An ordinary enough occurrence, but one which was to change his life, because the letter was from Suzanne Anderson who had got his name from *Dateline*.'
>
> *Dateline*

a Which words indicate the first-person viewpoint in *The Scarlet Thread* passage? Now rewrite the passage in the third person. How does an outsider's viewpoint affect the sense?

b What are the various ways you can tell that the *Dateline* passage is written by an outside narrator? Rewrite this passage in the first person as if you were Tim. How does a personal viewpoint alter the sense?

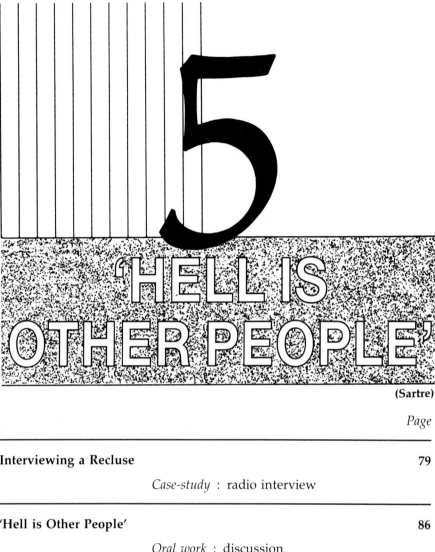

5

'HELL IS OTHER PEOPLE'

(Sartre)

INTERVIEWING A RECLUSE

She wants to be alone ...

In an age where social contact is not just encouraged but considered to be important in the preservation of sanity, the recluse exercises a peculiar and morbid fascination – particularly if he or she is wealthy or in some way celebrated. An investigation into the motives, whereabouts and foibles of the world's most notable and successful recluses.

Report by Russell Miller

When the world's most famous recluse, Howard Hughes, died in April, 1976, on an aeroplane flying him from Acapulco to Houston for medical treatment, the full horror of his descent into madness had still to be revealed. Yet ever since going into complete seclusion in 1950, he had been the subject of continual prurient interest.

Hughes could easily have found the privacy he craved by retiring, or quietly running his business interests from the back seat. Instead, he chose to slam the shutters on the world: labelled as a recluse, he instantly aroused public curiosity and thus, paradoxically, invited unwelcome attention.

In New York, an elderly woman steps out of an apartment block on East 52nd Street. She wears a nondescript raincoat, her grey hair tied back with a rubber band, a woollen hat pulled down over her ears and dark glasses. There is nothing to distinguish her from any other New Yorker out for a walk, but shopkeepers wink at their customers as she passes, joggers stop and stare. No one dares approach her, for everyone knows she is unapproachable – Garbo. Even that old matinee idol Rex Harrison, who lives in the apartment above Greta Garbo in New York, admits glumly: "She is unvisitable, poor darling."

Recluses have always held a peculiar fascination. The reason, says psychologist Dr Paul Brown, is that the great majority of people find isolation so uncomfortable that they go to enormous lengths to avoid it.

'One of the few things common to all human beings is that we are filling up time. We are either hunting for intimacy or trying to avoid isolation. We are social animals.

'At the same time, there are clearly some people who find contact with other human beings so threatening or so invasive that they feel the only safe thing to do is to prevent it happening. The particular reasons why a person wilfully decides to withdraw would be unique and could only be understood in relation to that person's psychological development. In the case of the Howard Hugheses of this world one could say there is plenty of evidence of the schizophrenic process.

'Some recluses are clearly clinically ill. Most of the time the world is just about a manageable place for most of us, but depression gives one an enormous sense of how puny one is and typically in a depressed state people feel the burdens they carry are too painful to deal with.

'Escaping some burden is the common theme, particularly for people in the public eye. We know, for example, that creating film stars is a process in which huge numbers of people have vested interests. The film star is the recipient of everyone else's ambition and that must be an intolerable task at times, difficult to survive if one is a fragile kind of person. Bette Davis's solution was to become an alcoholic – alcoholism is a way of withdrawing inasmuch as one becomes inaccessible.

'It is also quite common for one partner to withdraw after the death of the other. Salvador Dali did not become a recluse until after the death of his wife.'

Psychiatrist and psychotherapist Dr Glin Bennet made a special study of adult isolation and reported in a book, *Beyond Endurance*: 'If the external circumstances are too threatening, if the individual is experiencing a high degree of anxiety or is of an unstable temperament (to use that term rather loosely), then removing the reassuring presence of others may be catastrophic ... An extreme sense of isolation and abandonment is probably too much to expect any ordinary person to bear.'

He cites the pressures generated by success as a primary reason why so many celebrities in all fields choose to hide from the world. 'Success creates enormous problems that can become overwhelming: it's a very narrow perch at the top and someone is always trying to push you off. If you are very much celebrated you are expected to keep on scoring goals and amazing your followers. The halting of the creative flow and isolation often go hand in hand – Rossini, for example, became a recluse after he found he could no longer work.'

By their very nature, recluses are rarely willing to explain the reasons why they choose their own company, but it seems unlikely that they would admit to any particular eccentricity.

The only interview Garbo has ever given in the past 30 years, published in 1977 by a West German magazine, failed to shed light on her desire for seclusion. 'I'm restless everywhere and unable to settle down,' she is reported to have said. 'I think I always have been ... if only I knew where to go.'

The Sunday Times
20 July 1986

GRETA GARBO

Nearly 50 years ago, Greta Garbo supposedly said: 'I want to be alone.' She actually *said: 'I want to be left alone' – and she created the legend of the mysterious, reclusive film star, her allure made ever more tantalising by her withdrawal into solitude. She lives in an apartment overlooking the East River in New York, never entertains, never gives interviews, never shows any indication that she wants for anything other than to be left alone. The star of* Camille, Mata Hari *and* Anna Karenina *has lived in seclusion for nearly half a century, spurning all the trappings of stardom and approaches from the outside world. A Japanese paparazzo photographer has been waiting outside her apartment for more than three years, but has never succeeded in getting a full-face picture. Garbo's seclusion has done nothing to diminish the interest, and her 80th birthday last year was marked by fulsome tributes in newspapers all over the world – to which she contributed not a single word.*

MICHAEL JACKSON

Like many famous stars past and present, Michael Jackson has a highly reclusive life style. His home, a mock Tudor mansion, is protected by an iron gate, a guardhouse and a TV camera that surveys the long driveway. But Michael Jackson has also become increasingly reclusive by temperament. He appears to have few close friends and spends most of his time alone at home. Described as a prince in an ivory tower with no one to share his success with, his habits have become ever more eccentric. His home houses a gallery of shop dummies and life-size wax figures (including one of himself), with whom he is said to hold conversations. He also has a collection of 'pets' – plush toys named after the real-life animals kept in a small zoo in his 90 acre back garden. Extensive plastic surgery has given him an effeminate, fantastical appearance like a prince from a fairy-tale. In recent concert tours, his magical acts have helped to reinforce his self-image as a spirit from another world.

J. D. SALINGER

Aged 61, believed to be living near Windsor, Vermont, J. D. Salinger is still writing busily, although not for publication. His classic novel Catcher In The Rye, *published in 1951, spoke for a generation as eloquently as Hemingway and Fitzgerald and established him as one of the century's most gifted and original writers. Almost as soon as his work received major critical and popular recognition, Salinger retreated into silent self-communing. He has published nothing for more than 20 years and almost nothing is known about his life apart from odd autobiographical scraps picked up from his short stories in* The New Yorker. *His hermit-like seclusion and fanatical defence of his privacy is now so well-established that it is noted in his entry in the* Encyclopaedia Britannica, *which reports that he is increasingly preoccupied with mystical religious experience.*

SALVADOR DALI

The surrealist genius, now aged 81, retreated to a medieval castle at Pubol, on the north-east coast of Spain, after the death of his wife, Gala, in 1981. For more than two years, Dali remained behind closed shutters in a single room in the castle, cared for by two nurses and a handful of aides, completely cut off from the world. In August 1984, he was badly burned in a fire and taken to hospital in Barcelona, where doctors were shocked to discover he was suffering from extreme malnutrition – he weighed only 99lb – and was on the verge of death. Uneasy parallels were drawn with Howard Hughes as details emerged of Dali's self-imposed isolation, and rumours circulated that he was being manipulated by those people closest to him. The artist recovered from his burns and now lives in the tower of the museum he established at his birthplace, Figueras.

JEAN PAUL GETTY II

In July, 1971, Paul Getty's beautiful wife, Talitha, was found dead from a heroin overdose in their apartment in Rome. Fearing the police would implicate him in her death when they discovered he was also a heroin addict, Getty fled from Italy. He moved into a large, gloomy house in Cheyne Walk, Chelsea, and literally closed the shutters on life. For more than a decade he nursed his grief, turning away visitors and rarely emerging from the house except at night. Even when his son and namesake was kidnapped in Italy and later suffered a devastating stroke, Getty could not be persuaded to leave Cheyne Walk. Recently recovered from drug addiction, he is now intent on giving away his share of the vast Getty fortune, but he remains as shy and reclusive as ever, despite being recently awarded the KBE.

BOBBY FISCHER

Elusive wunderkind of American chess, Bobby Fischer turned and fled from his success more than 10 years ago after snatching the world chess crown from the Soviets in a series of dazzling games still re-played by admirers everywhere. He now hides behind an alias and lives in cheap hotels and bedsits in Pasadena, California, rarely emerging by day, but venturing out at night to distribute religious tracts under the windscreen wipers of parked cars. Always unorthodox and eccentric, he believes he is under KGB surveillance and is obsessed with a theory of world dominance by Soviet Jews. Only 43 years old, still considered the finest chess mind of his generation, few experts believe he will ever play again in public. He has consistently turned down sponsorship offers worth millions of dollars and is now said to live "hand to mouth".

MARLENE DIETRICH

In a fourth-floor apartment on the Avenue Montaigne in Paris, Marlene Dietrich spends most of her time on the telephone, writing letters on a portable typewriter and cleaning the floor on her hands and knees, swearing frequently in Yiddish. She has not performed in public since an accident backstage in Australia in 1975, when she fell and broke her hip. Now she turns down all offers and has made herself a prisoner in her own home, rarely venturing into the street for fear of being photographed. She still owns a luxurious apartment in Park Avenue, New York, but she has not been inside the door for years. When her friend Maximilian Schell asked to film an interview with her at home she refused, telling him: 'No one will ever trespass on my private world.' Last year, the 81-year-old star successfully sued an author and publisher, claiming that the foreword to a book of photographs devoted to her career intruded on her privacy.

For this Case-study, it will be useful to have studied the sections on Interviewing and Role-play in chapter 2.

A world famous recluse has agreed to allow a BBC Radio presenter to record an exclusive one-off interview. This will be part of a series of interviews of famous personalities called 'First Person'. You will be working in pairs to produce this 'radio programme' either as a tape-recorded interview or 'live' before your class.

1 Preparing your thoughts

a Read all the case-study material through carefully, both the article and the profiles of famous recluses.
b In your pair, think more closely about why people become recluses, by discussing the following questions.
  – What seems to be the typical behaviour of a recluse?
  – Why do psychologists consider the behaviour of recluses to be abnormal?
  – Why do successful people become recluses?
  – Look at the cases of *three* famous recluses. Why do you think each of these people became recluses?
  – Why is the public fascinated by famous recluses?
c In your pair, choose the recluse who interests both of you the most. If possible, do some further research into the life and background of this person, using the library and the knowledge of your friends or parents.

2 Preparing your roles

Now choose one of the two roles below:

Radio presenter

As the presenter of the radio programme 'First Person', you will be conducting a studio interview with the famous recluse, lasting no longer than ten minutes.
a Begin preparing your role by studying the case-study article and profile, and also by drawing on any background information you have found out about the recluse. Use all this information to work out a set of interview questions on the life, personality and motivation of your recluse, which you feel should satisfy the curiosity of the programme's listeners. (See the role of the *Recluse*.)
b Work out how you are going to conduct the interview. A recluse is likely to be more withdrawn than other people. How will you phrase your questions so that the recluse responds positively to you?

c Write an introduction to the interview (bearing in mind that this programme is one of a series on famous personalities), and also a brief conclusion.

Recluse

In your role as a famous recluse, you have decided to break your long silence on this one occasion, and speak to BBC Radio.

a Prepare your thoughts for the interview both by drawing on any background information you may have found out about the recluse you are impersonating and by imagining his or her life. Jot down notes on the following:
  – motives: reasons for becoming and staying a recluse;
  – feelings about your past life (before becoming a recluse);
  – reasons for talking now;
  – daily life style, contacts with people;
  – present fears, phobias, hopes.

b Decide how you will act in the interview. To what extent will you be forthcoming about yourself? To what extent reserved and secretive?

3 The interview

a When both of you have prepared your roles for the interview, decide how to conduct the interview. Will you rehearse it first? Or will you conduct the interview 'live'?

b Then produce your radio programme either as a tape-recording or 'live' before a studio audience – your class.

'HELL IS OTHER PEOPLE'

When the Tourists Flew In

The Finance Minister said
    'It will boost the economy
    the dollars will flow in.'

The Minister of Interior said
    'It will provide full
    and varied employment .
    for the indigenes.'

The Ministry of Culture said
    'It will enrich our life ...
    contact with other cultures
    must surely
    improve the texture of living.'

The man from the Hilton said
    'We will make you
    a second Paradise;
    for you, it is the dawn
    of a glorious new beginning!'

When the tourists flew in
    our island people
    metamorphosed into
    a grotesque carnival
    – a two-week sideshow

When the tourists flew in
    our men put aside
    their fishing nets
    to become waiters
    our women became whores

When the tourists flew in
    what culture we had
    flew out of the window
    we traded our customs
    for sunglasses and pop
    we turned sacred ceremonies
    into ten-cent peep shows

When the tourists flew in
    local food became scarce
    prices went up
    but our wages stayed low

When the tourists flew in
    we could no longer
    go down to our beaches
    the hotel manager said
    'Natives defile the sea-shore'

When the tourists flew in
    the hunger and the squalor
    were preserved
    as a passing pageant
    for clicking cameras
    – a chic eye-sore!

When the tourists flew in
    we were asked
    to be 'side-walk ambassadors'
    to stay smiling and polite
    to always guide
    the 'lost' visitor ...
    Hell, if we could only tell them
    where we really want them to go!

Cecil Rajendra

Benidorm 1962

Benidorm 1986

Request Stop

A queue at a Request Bus Stop. A WOMAN *at the head, with a* SMALL MAN *in a raincoat next to her, two other* WOMEN *and a* MAN.

WOMAN [*to* SMALL MAN]   'I beg your pardon, what did you say?

Pause.

All I asked you was if I could get a bus from here to Shepherds Bush.

Pause.

Nobody asked you to start making insinuations.

Pause.

Who do you think you are?

Pause.

Huh. I know your sort, I know your type. Don't worry, I know all about people like you.

Pause.

We can all tell where you come from. They're putting your sort inside every day of the week.

Pause.

All I've got to do, is report you, and you'd be standing in the dock in next to no time. One of my best friends is a plain-clothes detective.

Pause.

I know all about it. Standing there as if butter wouldn't melt in your mouth. Meet you in a dark alley it'd be ... another story. [*To the others, who stare into space.*] You heard what this man said to me. All I asked him was if I could get a bus from here to Shepherds Bush. [*To him.*] I've got witnesses, don't you worry about that.

Pause.

Impertinence.

Pause.

Ask a man a civil question he treats you like a threepenny bit. [*To him.*] I've got better things to do, my lad, I can assure you. I'm not going to stand here and be insulted on a public highway. Anyone can tell you're a foreigner. I was born just around the corner. Anyone can tell you're just up from the country for a bit of a lark. I know your sort.

Pause.

She goes to a LADY

Excuse me, lady. I'm thinking of taking this man up to the magistrate's court, you heard him make that crack, would you like to be a witness?

The LADY *steps into the road.*

LADY: Taxi . . .

She disappears..

WOMAN: We know what sort she is. [*Back to position.*] I was the first in this queue.

Pause.

Born just round the corner. Born and bred. These people from the country haven't the faintest idea of how to behave. Peruvians. You're bloody lucky I don't put you on a charge. You ask a straightforward question –

The others suddenly thrust out their arms at a passing bus. They run off left after it. The WOMAN, *alone, clicks her teeth and mutters. A man walks from the right to the stop, and waits. She looks at him out of the corner of her eye. At length she speaks shyly, hesitantly, with a slight smile.*

Excuse me. Do you know if I can get a bus from here . . . to Marble Arch?

Harold Pinter

Banished to Brandfort

'When they send me into exile, it's not me as an individual they are sending. They think that with me they can also ban the political ideas ... I couldn't think of a greater honour.'

Winnie Mandela (wife of Nelson Mandela, both leaders of the anti-apartheid movement in South Africa), was 'banished' from her home town of Orlando in 1977 for political activism. She was conveyed many miles away to Brandfort, a remote ghetto town for poor blacks. The banishment order contained a long list of restrictions upon her freedom. Among these, she was not allowed to:
– leave Brandfort without special permission;
– be with more than one person at a time;
– attend or address a public meeting;
– attend church without a permit;
– attend a college or university;
– enter any premises used for printing and publishing;
– enter a nursery, school or factory.

The following passage from her autobiography *Part of My Soul* tells of her surprise arrest and banishment.

It was the night of 16 May 1977. I was doing an assignment in sociology and, because I was working, I used to do my assignments at night – it took me right up to 2 am. There was a deadline. I had to submit something the following day. So I finished it at about half past two.

I had been hearing strange noises outside. But then it's such a usual part of my life, that kind of thing. I've always known that I'm never alone wherever I am, so hearing footsteps outside was nothing new; I've lived like that with these people, I just thought the police were making their usual rounds outside. I switched off the lights but I couldn't fall asleep.

At about four o'clock in the morning I heard a great noise outside – it seemed as if a hail of stones were dropped on my house and it sounded as if they were falling inside the wall – I've got this high cement wall around the house in Orlando.

In a fraction of a second there were knocks all over, on the doors, on all the windows, bang, bang, bang, bang-sounds. You would think they would ring the bell – no – simultaneous knocking on the door, barking, then I knew what was happening. I just took it for granted that I was under arrest. I thought as usual they were taking me under Section 6. [The section of the Terrorism Act under which Winnie Mandela was held in 1969. It provided for indefinite, incommunicado detention while under interrogation.]

I went and opened the door and of course I saw the whole army inside the yard, chaps in camouflage carrying guns, and members of the Security Branch; they were all heavily armed.

I always keep a suitcase packed with clothes because of the problems I've had in the past. I've always been detained alone – my children were usually in boarding schools. I have a suitcase ready, so that when I'm taken to prison nobody is going to have to struggle to find me – I have a set of clothes, toiletry, toothbrushes, combs.

I picked up that case. And then they said, 'You are under arrest.' There was the usual angry exchange. My daughter Zindzi was with me, and I wasn't prepared to leave her without exactly knowing how long I would be away. I never even had time to finish – I was whisked away, then I was taken to Protea police station.

There they tried to interrogate me, but if you have been inside as long as I have, you cannot go through that worthless exercise again. No policeman can come to me today at my age and think that he can still interrogate me. In my younger days it was different, but any squeak of a little policeman who came to question me today would just be wasting his time. We would just end up insulting each other, that's all. This went on for the rest of the morning till about ten o'clock. At ten o'clock I saw Zindzi escorted into the cell I was kept in with these heavily armed chaps, and she was carrying the house keys. And for the first time I realized what was happening. These three men who were in the same cell interrogating me simply stood up and said, 'You are now going to be banished to the Free State.' I hadn't the slightest idea of what was going on, I thought I was under arrest. From there I thought I was going to be moved either to Pretoria or to another of the country's prisons as usual. And when Zindzi came with these men it was the first time I realized I was being banished.

We were taken into one of these army trucks. Our every possession was there: they had ripped off bedspreads and sheets from the bed, they took everything, emptied the wardrobes and cupboards into those sheets, my crockery was tied up with the blankets, three quarters of course was broken into pieces, Nelson's books were bundled into bedspreads. Of course half the stuff got damaged.

Then we drove to the Free State, just like that. Zindzi and I were at the back between heavily armed men and there were others in front. And then of course there were other trucks escorting us. I had never even known that there was a place like Brandfort. We were dropped at the police station and handed over to the Security Branch of the Free State. They were all there in full force too.

From there we were driven to the house – in fact it's an insult to call these three cells a house – when we got there, there wasn't even room to enter – the soil took up three quarters of each little cell. They had to get men with shovels to scoop the soil from the rooms, they were so full of rubbish. What we subsequently gathered from the neighbourhood was that when they were building the so-called new houses for the area, the builders used that house for dumping all their rubbish. They threw some of our bundles on the floor; they couldn't get one single item of our furniture through the doors. Apparently the little doors that are used for these houses are what you normally use for toilets – that is why our furniture got stored at the police station.

That first night naturally we hadn't washed, there isn't a drop of water – suddenly our house in Soweto seemed like a palace; we didn't have a bucket, not even a morsel of food. We couldn't cook. There was no stove. We were just dumped between these four walls. It was bitterly cold. We cuddled up on one mattress to get some sleep. It was terrible. For Zindzi it was a traumatic experience. Any man could have been broken by that type of thing. It was calculated to do just that. Worse things have happened to people in the struggle, but for a sixteen-year-old girl it was very hard to take. It was the hardest thing for me to take as a mother, that your commitment affects those who are very dear to you. That shattering experience inflicted a wound that will never heal. Of course I was bitter, more than I've ever been.

At first the people in the location were petrified. The so-called Members of Parliament around here and the police had held meetings, and the people had been told that a big communist was coming and they were warned of the dangers of associating with such a person. They were told this is a woman who is going to tell you that you must fight for your land, she is going to tell you all the wrong things. And if ever you set a foot in her house, we will promptly arrest you and you will spend the rest of your life like her husband, whom we arrested and who is in prison for life. And they were told to restrain their children and when they send their children to the shops they must see to it that they don't come anywhere near the house.

But today the black thinking is: if a white man says something is bad, then it must be very good. Although they were frightened by that type of thing, it was the exact opposite. This has been the pattern with all these racial laws anyway. Once a black is told by a white man that something is bad, then it must be good and vice versa. That's what happened. We didn't have any bridges to build. As time went on, people came to know who we were and what the whole thing was all about – we never addressed the people. Little children started spontaneously giving the Black Power sign, that is how they greeted us when the police were gone. They would wake us up early in the morning and bring us little parcels of food – some beans or cabbage – of course during the day nobody would speak to us. But at night they came and expressed their solidarity. That's what happened.

And every one of them knew of Nelson. Every one of them.

I have ceased a long time ago to exist as an individual. The ideals, the political goals that I stand for, those are the ideals and goals of the people in this country. They cannot just forget their own ideals. My private self doesn't exist. Whatever they do to me, they do to the people in this country. I am and will always be only a political barometer. From every situation I have found myself in, you can read the political heat in the country at a particular time. When they send me into exile, it's not me as an individual they are sending. They think that with me they can also ban the political ideas. But that is a historical impossibility. They will never succeed in doing that. I am of no importance to them as an individual. What I stand for is what they want to banish. I couldn't think of a greater honour.

Prayer Before Birth

I am not yet born; O hear me.
Let not the bloodsucking bat or the rat or the stoat or the
   club-footed ghoul come near me.

I am not yet born, console me.
I fear that the human race may with tall walls wall me,
   with strong drugs dope me, with wise lies lure me,
      on black racks rack me, in blood-baths roll me.

I am not yet born; provide me
With water to dandle me, grass to grow for me, trees to talk
   to me, sky to sing to me, birds and a white light
      in the back of my mind to guide me.

I am not yet born; forgive me
For the sins that in me the world shall commit, my words
   when they speak me, my thoughts when they think me,
      my treason engendered by traitors beyond me,
         my life when they murder by means of my
            hands, my death when they live me.

I am not yet born; rehearse me
In the parts I must play and the cues I must take when
   old men lecture me, bureaucrats hector me, mountains
      frown at me, lovers laugh at me, the white
         waves call me to folly and the desert calls
            me to doom and the beggar refuses
               my gift and my children curse me.

I am not yet born; O hear me,
Let not the man who is beast or who thinks he is God
   come near me.

I am not yet born; O fill me
With strength against those who would freeze my
   humanity, would dragoon me into a lethal automaton,
      would make me a cog in a machine, a thing with
         one face, a thing, and against all those
            who would dissipate my entirety, would
               blow me like thistledown hither and
                  thither or hither and thither
                    like water held in the
                      hands would spill me.

Let them not make me a stone and let them not spill me.
Otherwise kill me.

Louis MacNeice

When the Tourists Flew In

Discussion

1 Where in the world might this island be? Are you given any clues in the poem?

2 Before tourism arrived at the island, what do we learn about:
   – the way the islanders made a living;
   – their standard of living;
   – their life style and customs?

3 What changes do you gather tourism has brought to these features of people's lives?

4 How would you summarise Cecil Rajendra's objections to tourism? For example, is Rajendra saying that there were no problems on the island before tourism?

5 Have you any experience of a place or a country which you consider has been harmed by tourism?

Writing

1 Write two or more stanzas for the poem either beginning with a line such as:
   'Our Chief of Police said . . .'
   'Our President said . . .'
   'Our Ministry of Welfare said . . .'

   or, beginning with a line such as:
   'When the tourists flew in,
   our children . . .
   our homes . . .
   the land . . .
   our old people . . .'

2 Design an advertisement for a holiday brochure, which deliberately disguises the bad effects tourism is having on the island. In writing this, try to adopt a tourist's eye view of such features as:
   – the natural beauty of sea and countryside;
   – the local culture, history and customs;
   – the hotel and restaurant facilities, and so on.
   (See chapter 9 on Advertising language).

3 Write a strong letter of protest from Cecil Rajendra, an active human rights campaigner, to one of our national papers, against the effects of tourism on people's lives on the island. The main purpose of the letter is to publicise the damage tourism has done to the island's environment and way of life, in order to deter people from holidaying there. Perhaps describe what the island was like before the arrival of tourism and contrast this with the life there now.

Discussion

'Request Stop' is a monologue – a play in which only one character, a woman, speaks.

1 Choose a confident volunteer to read this aloud. Then read the play through again, this time on your own, asking yourself what you learn about the woman character.

2 In pairs, study both what the woman says, as well as the way she says it, to create a character sketch of her. Make notes on what you consider to be:
    – the woman's appearance: her age, height, build, facial features, hairstyle and dress
    – the sound of her voice: for example, her regional dialect or accent
    – her way of life
    – her fears and insecurities (her attitude to other people, for instance).

3 As a class, compare your character sketches. Where you disagree with others, can you find evidence from the play to support your vision of this woman?

Role-play/creative writing

1 The Small Man's Thoughts

Who is the small man and what is he really thinking? In pairs, add to Pinter's script by imagining and writing in the small man's thoughts as the woman rants at him. Use the stage direction 'Pause', as the cue for the small man's responses. Perhaps act out or tape record the 'dialogue' between the woman's speeches and the small man's 'asides'.

2 A Woman Rants . . .

Imagine this same woman (or an equivalent man) in one of the following situations:

a In a doctor's waiting room, picking on the National Health Service.
b In a supermarket queue, ranting about big shopping stores, their food prices and quality.
c In a launderette, picking on a particular issue, such as: the young, the media, people on strike, etc.
d In the social security office ranting about welfare officers, social workers and so on.

In pairs, work out a scene between your character and an unfortunate bystander based on one of the situations above, or similar. Choose whether you use a monologue format like the Pinter play, or whether you opt for some response (perhaps spoken or unspoken asides) from your bystander.

   Like Pinter, try to build up the character's obsession with the chosen subject gradually, until the remarks become so extreme that a change of circumstances has to occur. Then the situation can begin all over again.

<table>
<tr><td>'Banished to Brandfort'</td></tr>
</table>

Discussion and understanding

1 From your reading of the passage, what do you gather Winnie Mandela has done to deserve 'banishment' from her home in Orlando?

2 Read the first two paragraphs carefully. From the way they are written, how can we tell that something is going to happen to Winnie?

3 What evidence is there in the descriptions of Winnie's arrest and interrogation that she is used to being harassed by the police?

4 Find five examples from the passage of police methods which Winnie considers to be excessive or unnecessarily rough.

5 How is Winnie's great sense of bitterness shown in the way that she describes the new house in Brandfort? Pick out descriptive words or phrases which indicate her bitterness.

6 *a* What do you understand by Winnie's description of herself in the last paragraph as 'only a political barometer'?
   b Explain what Winnie means when she says of her banishment, 'I couldn't think of a greater honour'.

7 *a* What negative attitudes and feelings do you think the passage shows between people? Can you explain the causes of this?
   b What positive attitudes and feelings are shown between people in the passage?

Drawing on any knowledge you may have of the political situation in South Africa today, do you think that life for Winnie Mandela is likely to have improved?

Creative writing

1 After her arrival in Brandfort, Winnie Mandela contravened her banishment order on many occasions. Usually, she was arrested then released, as the authorities were aware of her influence on public opinion both at home and abroad.
   Imagine one of these occasions and write a scene for a play script in which Winnie is interrogated by the police. Draw fully on what you have learnt about her personality and her experience of the police.

2 Tell the story of Winnie's arrival in Brandfort and its likely consequences, through the eyes of *one* of the following people:
   – Zindzi, her daughter
   – a member of the Security police responsible for watching her
   – a neighbour, aware of her reputation.

Reading aloud

The poem is a dramatic monologue spoken by an unborn child. To help appreciate its meaning, try reading the poem aloud. It has a strong, pulsating rhythm like a heartbeat and in places, the words echo each other in rhyme (e.g. 'bat' and 'rat' in the second line).

1   In groups of about four, experiment with reading this poem aloud. Make use of all your voices and perhaps try some of these variations:
    – each person in turn reads a stanza;
    – the first line of each stanza is read by the group in chorus, the rest by each person in turn;
    – the opposite to this: i.e. first line by one person, the rest by the group;
    – key words in a line are read in chorus, the rest by one person: e.g. 'Let not the *blood*sucking *bat* or the *rat* or the *stoat* or the *club*-footed *ghoul* come near me.'

2   Then when you are satisfied with your group reading, recite your version to the class or, perhaps, tape-record it.

Poem appreciation

1   What do you think the poem is about?

2   The poem is full of words to do with 'nature' and 'civilisation'. Using a chart like the one below, note down all the words from each stanza associated with one category or the other. In addition, note whether the word connotes a good thing to the unborn child, or a bad:

	Nature	Civilisation
'Good'	e.g. Water	
'Bad'		e.g. Drugs

What do you notice about the type of words used to connote 'good' things? And 'bad' things? Do some words have both 'good' and 'bad' meanings? Why might this be?

3   Each stanza describes either the child's fears and future sins or its hopes. For each stanza, try to think of examples from real life, past or present, of people to whom the description has applied (or may apply now); e.g. 'the bloodsucking bat' and so on, could be seen as the fears of primitive tribes or of children.

4   For a closer study of the use of poetic language in this poem, use the guidance given in *Techniques*: 'Appreciating poetry'.

Appreciating poetry

This section will help you to make a critical study of any poem in this book or, indeed, elsewhere. In particular it supports the activity work for Louis MacNeice's 'Prayer before Birth'.

Poetry appreciation means studying a poem not simply to understand its meaning but also to appreciate *how* the poet uses language to say something to the reader. Poems do not have one right meaning which your teacher mysteriously knows and you do not. The value of poetry lies in your own response to a poem – your personal understanding of it. However, you can guide yourself into a fuller appreciation of poetry simply by knowing more about a poet's craft. This section identifies some of the ways poets use language to create a poem's meaning.

1 Form

All poems have a form – that is an overall structure, which shapes and organises its meaning. Much traditional poetry was written in well-known and much-used verse forms, such as the sonnet, the ballad and the epic poem. These verse forms determined such things as the number of lines in a poem, the length of each line, and the type of rhyme and rhythm. Many modern poets do not follow such conventions, but allow the meaning of a particular poem to determine its form.

- In 'Prayer Before Birth', notice that the poem has an unusual form: in general, each stanza gets longer and from the second line within each stanza, each line gets shorter. From your reading of the poem, can you suggest why MacNeice has chosen this particular form?

2 Sound effects

Most poetry is written to be read aloud – it is like a spoken version of music. It is the pattern of sounds which governs the order and arrangement of words in each line, and of sentences in each stanza. Indeed, the meaning of a poem may only become clear when it is read aloud. Here are some of the ways in which poetry creates a kind of spoken music.

Rhythm As in music, rhythm is simply the pattern of beats or stresses upon words or word syllables. Much traditional poetry is 'stress syllable' verse: that is, verse which combines a count of stresses and syllables in each line to give a recognisable rhythm. For example, syllables in a line might be alternately stressed then unstressed. In modern poetry, the rhythm is freer and less calculated.

- In 'Prayer Before Birth', there is no set rhythm, but when you read it aloud, you will find that your voice naturally emphasises certain words or syllables and runs lightly over others. For example in ll. 2–3:

    'Lét not the blóodsucking bát or the rát or the stóat or the clúb-footed ghóul come neár me.'

- Select another stanza and work out where the strong beats seem to fall. How does the pattern of stresses help the meaning in your chosen stanza?

Rhyme   For many people, the distinguishing feature of poetry is rhyme – perhaps because of our common experience of nursery rhymes. Rhyme is where the end of a word or group of words exactly echoes the sound of another. It is used fairly commonly in traditional poetry, to achieve a predictable sound pattern at the end of each line.

Although some modern poems use end-of-line rhyme, many others in preference use *internal rhyme* – that is, rhyme within the line. There are two common types of internal rhyme:

Alliteration : this is where the first letter of two or more words in a line are repeated to give emphasis to their sense, for example in stanza 2, line 3 of 'Prayer Before Birth':

   'with strong *d*rugs *d*ope me, with wise *l*ies *l*ure me'.

Assonance : this is where the vowel sound of a word echoes another in the same line or close to it, for example in stanza 2, line 4:

   'bl*ack* r*acks* r*ack* me'

- Identify every instance of alliteration and assonance in stanza 2. How does the strong use of internal rhyme help to emphasise the theme of this stanza?

3 Imagery

Imagery is a comparison of one thing with another. It is used in poetry, as in all writing, to stimulate your imagination, and to enlarge your perception of the thing being compared. Two main types of imagery are *simile* and *metaphor* (See *Techniques*: 'Describing people', chapter 3, which deals with this in more detail.)

Simile is where one thing is compared to something else, using the words 'like' or 'as'.

Metaphor is where one thing *is* another thing: the comparison is not made explicit.

- In stanza 7 of 'Prayer Before Birth', see if you can identify examples of both simile and metaphor.

In fact, 'Prayer Before Birth' really works beyond the level of simile and metaphor – it is as though the whole poem is written in imagery, at a *symbolic* level. Of course you can take the poem at face value – if the unborn child could see into its future, it really might fear bats, drugs, sinning, mountains and the machine age. But its fears, both concrete and abstract, also *symbolise* those of humanity through the ages. (See point 3 in the 'Poem Appreciation' exercise.)

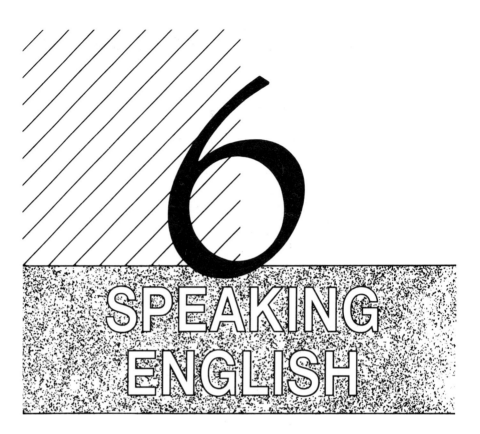

6

SPEAKING ENGLISH

ENGLISH DIALECTS

Dahn the Plug 'Ole

A muvver was barfin' 'er biby one night,
The youngest of ten and a tiny young mite,
The muvver was poor and the biby was thin,
Only a skelington covered in skin;
The muvver turned rahnd for the soap off the rack,
She was but a moment, but when she turned back,
The biby was gorn; and in anguish she cried,
'Oh, where is my biby?' – The angels replied:

'Your biby 'as fell dahn the plug 'ole,
Your biby 'as gorn dahn the plug;
The poor little thing was so skinny and thin
'E oughter been barfed in a jug;
Your biby is perfeckly 'appy,
'E won't need a barf any more,
Your biby 'as fell dahn the plug 'ole
Not lorst, but gorn before.'

(anon.)

Fraffly Posh

This is a conversation between a posh-sounding colonel in the army and a posh-sounding lady who has invited him to tea. The colonel is complaining about a man he doesn't like.

Demmortol Mogret, chep zirnia winker monda. Snort ziffy was an F.I. Smoshel. Feller rotterb cot moshelled. Gairdw do things bettrin the yommy. Arrer member beckon 47, or meffpin 48. Any wet was in Tripoli. No, meffpin nelleck-zendri-yaw ...

Earce. Ears of coss. End now, meddier Colonel, prep shoot lacquer little something tweet. Eddu wishooed trair little sneck. Arm shawr chewler gree wimmer steffer nother little toxoon. Shuggah?

adapted from *Fraffly Suite*, by Afferbeck Lauder

The Daughter-in-Law

In this extract from Act 2, Minnie and Luther, only recently married, are already having problems. Luther has spent the evening out without telling Minnie where he was going. He returns home 'rather tipsy' and inevitably they begin to quarrel.

[*She moves about; lays table for his morning's breakfast: a newspaper, cup, plate, etc. – no food, because it would go dry; rinses his tin pit-bottle, puts it and his snapbag on the table.*]

LUTHER	I could do it for mysen. Tha ned do nowt for me.
MINNIE	Why this sudden fit of unselfishness?
LUTHER	I niver want thee to do nowt for me, niver no more. No, not so much as lift a finger for me – not if I wor dyin'.
MINNIE	You're not dying; you're only tipsy.
LUTHER	Well, it's no matter to thee what I am.
MINNIE	It's very comfortable for you to think so.
LUTHER	I know nowt about that.
MINNIE	[*after a pause*] Where have you been to-night?
LUTHER	There an' back, to see how far it is.
MINNIE	[*making an effort*] Have you been up to your mother's?
LUTHER	Where I've bin, I've bin, and where I haven't, I haven't.
MINNIE	Pah! – you needn't try to magnify it and make a mountain. You've been to your mother's, and then to 'The Ram'.
LUTHER	All right – if tha knows, that knows, an' theer's an end on't.
MINNIE	You talk like a fool.
LUTHER	That comes o' bein' a fool.
MINNIE	When were you a fool?
LUTHER	Ivry day o' my life, an' ivry breath I've ta'en.
MINNIE	[*having finished work, sits down again*] I suppose you haven't got it in you to say anything fresh.
LUTHER	Why, what dost want me ter say ? [*He looks at her for the first time.*]
MINNIE	[*with a queer catch*] You might be more of a man if you said you were sorry.
LUTHER	Sorry! Sorry for what?
MINNIE	You've nothing to be sorry *for*, have you?
LUTHER	[*looking at her, quickly*] What art goin' ter say?
MINNIE	It's what are *you* going to say. [*A silence.*]
LUTHER	[*doggedly*] I'm goin' ter say nowt.
MINNIE	[*bitterly*] No, you're not *man* enough to say anything – you can only slobber. You do a woman a wrong, but you're never man enough to say you're sorry for it. You're *not* a man, you're not – you're something crawling!
LUTHER	I'm glad! I'm glad! I'm glad! No, an' I wouldna ta'e't back, no. 'Er wor nice wi' me, which is a thing tha's niver bin. An' so tha's got it, an' mun keep it.
MINNIE	Who was nice with you?
LUTHER	*She* was – an' would ha'e bin at this minnit, but for thee.
MINNIE	Pah! – you're not fit to have a wife. You only want your mother to rock you to sleep.

102

LUTHER   Neither mother, nor wife, neither thee nor onybody do I want – no – no.

MINNIE   No – you've had three cans of beer.

LUTHER   An' if ter niver sleeps i' th' bed wi' me again, an' if ter niver does a hand's turn for me niver no more, I'm glad, I'm glad. I non want thee. I non want ter see thee.

D. H. Lawrence

The Windae-Hingers

Two Glasgow housewives appear simultaneously at adjacent tenement windows which are wide open. Each is seated and her elbows are placed on a cushion on a window-sill.

SERAH   Did ye get home a'right fae the licensed grocers' dance?

MAGGIE   Aye, but Wullie strained his back helpin' me alang the street.

SERAH   Puir wee sowl. Ye shoulda took a taxi.

MAGGIE   Ach Ah wiz walkin' fine till Wullies lost his grip oan me.

SERAH   It's ages since there wiz ony excitement in the street.

MAGGIE   No' since yon night when Big Bella McLeish was threw oot the pub at the corner an'landit oan Wee Mrs McGravie.

SERAH   That Bella McLeish gives hur man the life o' a dug. She gives him Pal Meat an' egg fur his brekfast an' Pal Meat sangwidges fur his dinner an' tea.

MAGGIE   Aye, they say he ett that much Pal Meat he couldny pass a lamp-post.

SERAH   Oh therr's Michelle McGuffie. A nice wee lassie but she dizny look too weel.

MAGGIE   Naw she dizny. Hur murra got the doctor tae her. He tell't hur 'Ye canny expec' tae feel weel if ye work all day an' dance in the disco all night.' There was nothin' fur it, she hud tae gi'e up hur joab.

SERAH   Ah'm told she wiz engaged tae a young French fella she met in Majorca. He hud luvly manners. But every time he kissed hur hand he burnt his nose on her fag. Then wan day he went tae kiss her an' her bubblegum burst in his face. He began tae look down his nose at hur. So she broke it aff.

Stanley Baxter

103

No Dialects Please

This poem by Merle Collins who grew up in Grenada, is written in a mixture of Caribbean English and Standard British English.

In this competition
dey was looking for poetry of worth
for a writin that could wrap up a feelin
an fling it back hard
with a captive power to choke de stars
so dey say,
'Send them to us
but NO DIALECTS PLEASE'
We're British!

Ay!
Well ah laugh till me boushet near drop
Is not only dat ah tink
of de dialect of de Normans and de Saxons
dat combine an reformulate
to create a language-elect
is not only dat ah tink
how dis British education mus really be narrow
if it leave dem wid no knowledge
of what dey own history is about
is not only dat ah tink
bout de part of my story
dat come from Liverpool in a big dirty white ship
mark
AFRICAN SLAVES PLEASE!
We're the British!

But as if dat not enough pain
for a body to bear
ah tink bout de part on de plantations down dere
Wey dey so frighten o de power
in the deep spaces
behind our watching faces
dat dey shout
NO AFRICAN LANGUAGES PLEASE!
It's against the law!
Make me ha to go
an start up a language o me own
dat ah could share wid me people

Den when we start to shout
bout a culture o we own
a language o we own
a identity o we own
dem an de others dey leave to control us say
STOP THAT NONSENSE NOW
We're all British!
Every time we lif we foot to do we own ting
to fight we own fight
dey tell us how British we British
an ah wonder if dey remember
dat in Trinidad in the thirties
dey jail Butler*
who dey say is their British citizen
an accuse him of
Hampering the war effort!
Then it was
FIGHT FOR YOUR COUNTRY, FOLKS!
You're British!

Ay! Ay!
Ah wonder when it change to
NO DIALECTS PLEASE!
WE'RE British
Huh!
To tink how still dey so dunce
an so frighten o we power
dat dey have to hide behind a language
that we could wrap roun we little finger
in addition to we own!
Heavens o mercy!
Dat is dunceness oui!
Ah wonder where is de bright British?

Merle Collins

* Uriah (Buzz) Butler was a Grenadan who led a national strike for the rights of
workers in Trinidad at the start of the Second World War. He wanted fair conditions
for black workers in the British colonies, comparable to those granted to white
workers in the United Kingdom.

Reading aloud

In pairs, choose one of the following:

'Dahn the Plug 'Ole' : Cockney poem
'The Windae-Hingers' : Glaswegian conversation
'Fraffly Posh' : Posh-sounding conversation,

Together, work out a reading of the piece, trying to capture the dialect and character of the speaker(s). Then, either do a tape-recording of your reading, or do a 'live' reading before your class.

<table>
<tr><td>

The Daughter-in-Law

</td></tr>
</table>

Discussion and understanding

First, read the play extract through in pairs (male/female if possible). Allow at least two practice readings of the passage to get a feel for the Nottinghamshire dialect as well as for the personalities of Minnie and Luther. After this elect one pair to give their readings before the class. Then answer the following questions:

1 What do we gather Luther does for a living? What clues to this can you find in the extract?

2 What differences do you notice in the dialects of Minnie and Luther? How is this indicated in the way that the writer, D. H. Lawrence, has written what they say?

3 What do you learn of Luther's character? How do you feel towards him?

4 What effect does Luther's dialect have upon the way you view him as a character?
   To answer this, it may help to 'translate' his first six responses to Minnie into 'standard English'. If he spoke in standard English, would this alter the view you have of him at all?

5 For whom do you feel more sympathy in the marriage – Minnie or Luther? Is this feeling influenced by the way each one speaks?

<table>
<tr><td>

No Dialects Please!

</td></tr>
</table>

First read the poem through 'in your head' to understand the dialect and the subject matter. Then, either select someone in the class who is familiar with the dialect, to read the poem aloud. Or, in pairs, try reading the poem in two voices – one of you reading the Caribbean English, the other reading the white British slogans (in capital letters) and the following line. Then answer these questions:

1 The poetry competition rule, 'NO DIALECTS PLEASE!' implies a particular view of the English language. What is this?
   What do we learn about Merle Collins' own background which would make her critical of this view?

2 What would you say is Merle Collins' main feeling in this poem? How can you tell this from the way the poem is written?

3 What is the British attitude towards language and other aspects of life that she is criticising?

4 Merle Collins draws on a number of cases in British history to illustrate the attitude she is criticising. Explain why she draws on each of the following:
   – the history of the English language;
   – Britain's part in sending African slaves to work in their colonies in the West Indies, where African languages were banned;
   – the attempt of African slaves and their descendents to devise their own language (now known as 'creole' or 'patois');
   – Butler's part in helping West Indian workers just before the Second World War.

5 Why does the poet accuse the British of 'dunceness' at the end of the poem?

6 What do you think the poem might be saying about the political importance of language?

Writing

1 Write a dialect conversation between two local people from where you live. Choose topics of conversation reflecting the kind of interests, concerns or activities people have in your district. Your conversation could be written either as play script or in story form. (See *Techniques*: 'Writing dialogue', chapter 7.)

2 Write a dialect conversation between two people who come from a region or background other than your own. (Perhaps use one of the dialects in the reading materials you have studied).
   Your two characters could either share the same dialect, or have different dialects. Consider using any of these characters:

   A market stall holder   *A football supporter*
   A gossiping neighbour   *A stockbroker*
   A public school boy/girl   *An old-age pensioner*
   A Lord/Lady   *A cleaner*

3 Write an argument or a discussion essay on one of the following subjects:

   • 'Standard English is a tool used by the British establishment to make people conform.'

   • 'Dialects lead to a lack of understanding and toleration between people who are supposed to share a common language.'

Speaking English

Written English isn't a very good way of telling you how people actually sound when they speak.

- For example, if you heard people getting on a train in Glasgow, and then tried to write down the sentences you heard as they actually sound, you might get:

  'Huv ye no' brung the sangwidges?'
  ('*Haven't you brought the sandwiches?*')
  or:
  'Keepa haudera wean.'
  ('*Keep a hold of the wee one.*')

- How do the following sentences sound when you say them? If they are not the exact words you would use, change them. Then try them in a pair with one person saying the sentence and the other trying to write down the sounds *exactly*:

  'Hello. How are you? I'll see you later!'
  'Have you brought that letter with you?'
  'Get that great bag off my foot.'

You may find that people round you have *written* down the sentences in different ways. That's often because people *say* things in different ways. If everything was written down exactly as people spoke, then reading would be very difficult for everyone.

What affects the way people speak? Here are a few important factors:

1 Accent

An accent is the way you pronounce or lay stress on a particular word or part of a word. In practice, though, when you say that someone is speaking 'with an accent', you often mean more than this – a whole manner of speaking which is distinctive to a group of people or a region.

- Read the conversation 'Fraffly Posh' between the two posh-sounding people. If you have trouble, 'translate' it into English you understand. It is quite likely that the accent they use is different from your own!

2 Dialect

Quite often when people use the word 'accent' they really mean 'dialect'. A dialect is a form of language which is used in a particular district. The way you speak probably reflects the region in which you were brought up – unless, of course, you have moved around a lot. Not only will you pronounce words differently from people who live in other parts of the English-speaking world, but also you will also use a different grammar.

- For example, traditionally the Nottinghamshire dialect uses old forms of the English verb, for example Luther in 'The Daughter-in-Law':

  'Why what *dost* want me to say?'
  'What *art* going to say?'

Dialects also have their own special words, many of which may have become everyday speech for people from other regions. Look at these examples:
examples:

Cockney	Scottish	'Cowboy' American
squire	bairn	stampede
mate	burn	sombrero
titfer	bonny	rodeo
nosh	glen	desperado
buckshee	wee	bronco
trouble & strife	ken	lasso

- Now make a list of words and phrases for the region in which *you* live. If you come from a country or region listed above, add more examples to your list.

3 Standard English

This is the term used to describe the dialect of English which is officially used throughout the world for writing and printed materials. It has standard rules for grammar, punctuation and spelling. The English you write for coursework in school and college is all supposed to be in Standard English. However, it may be *spoken* with a variety of accents.

- Can you think of examples of errors in your use of Standard English, which you commonly make in your writing? Do any of these errors come from the English you use when you speak?

4 Received pronunciation

This is the accent of spoken English which is understood throughout the world. It is the accent frequently used in education and in broadcasting.

- Can you think of any well-known television newscaster who speaks with a regional accent?
- Which are the areas in television where regional accents are acceptable? Why is this?
- Do you agree with the value placed on a standard type of English and its pronunciation?

7

'BORN TO SET
IT RIGHT'

(Hamlet)

YOU AND YOUR RIGHTS

The Case-study material below is adapted from a pull-out section of 'Childright' – a monthly bulletin published by The Children's Legal Centre, who represent the rights of children and young people in England and Wales. For more detailed information, write to: The C.L.S., 20 Compton Terrace, London N1 2UN.

A year by year summary

You can:

- have an account in your name with a bank or building society, or have Premium Bonds in your name.
- have goods or money left to you.
- give or refuse consent to all health, dental and contraceptive treatment, provided you understand what this involves.
- complain if you feel discriminated against on the grounds of race, colour or nationality.
- open a bank account provided you understand what this involves.

You can:

- get free, full-time, state education.
- see a U or a PG category film at cinema unaccompanied.
- drink alcohol legally in private.

You can:

- draw money from your Post Office or TSB savings account.

You can:

- be detained by the police who can:
  – take your fingerprints
  – photograph you
  – take body samples.
- be taken into care if guilty of an offence.
- be convicted of a criminal offence (but until you are 14, the prosecution has to prove you know the difference between right and wrong).

You can:

- get a part-time job so long as it is a 'light' one for not more than two hours a day or one on Sundays.

You can:

- go into a pub but not drink or buy alcohol there.
- own an air rifle and, under certain circumstances, a shot gun.
- (boys) be found guilty of rape and unlawful sexual intercourse with a girl under 16. (Under 14, he is not considered physically capable).
- (boys) be sentenced to a detention centre.

You can:

- open a Post Office or a Girobank account but you'll need a guarantor – someone who will be liable for your debts.
- be given a youth custody sentence or (boys) be sent to prison to await trial if you've committed an offence.
- see a category 15 film.

You can:

- leave school.
- get a full-time job and join a Trades Union.
- get a National Insurance number.
- claim supplementary and social security benefits.
- leave home, usually with a parent's consent. (In law, you are in their custody until you're 18.)
- choose your own religion.
- (girls) consent to sexual intercourse.
- buy Premium Bonds.
- choose your own doctor and consent to medical, dental and contraceptive treatment.
- have to pay prescription charges.
- get a passport with your parent's signature on the application form.
- hold a licence to drive a moped, a motor-cycle, certain tractors and invalid cars.
- pay full fare on public transport.
- (boys) join the armed forces with your parents' consent.
- be used by another person to beg on the streets.
- enter a brothel and live there.
- drink beer, wine, cider or perry in a pub, hotel or restaurant if you're having a meal.
- buy cigarettes or tobacco.
- buy fireworks.

You can:

- no longer be received into care.
- be sent to prison if you are convicted of a serious crime.
- become a street trader.
- (girls) join the armed forces with parental consent at $17\frac{1}{2}$.
- hold a driving licence for all types of vehicles except heavy goods.
- buy or hire any firearm or ammunition with a licence.
- hold a pilot's licence and apply for a helicopter licence.

(You reach the age of majority – you are an adult in the eyes of the law.)

You can:

- vote in general and local elections.
- serve on a jury.
- leave home whether or not your parents agree.
- marry without your parents' or guardians' consent.
- open a bank account without a parent's signature and get a cheque card and credit card.
- buy on credit and get a mortgage.
- own land, property and shares in your own name.
- sign contracts, sue and be sued in the courts.
- make a will and act as an executor for someone else's will.
- see your birth certificate if you are adopted.
- apply for your own passport.
- change your name without your parents' consent.
- join the armed forces without your parents' consent.
- give blood.
- have to pay for dental treatment.
- be tattooed.
- donate your body to science.
- buy drinks in pubs and drink them there.
- work in a bar.
- see a category 18 film.

You can:

- stand for the local council or Parliament.
- adopt a child.
- (men) engage in homosexual activity in private if your partner is over 21.
- hold a licence to sell alcohol.
- be sentenced to life imprisonment if convicted of serious crimes.
- hold a licence to drive a lorry or a bus.

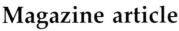

Magazine article

You are a member of the editorial team of your college or sixth-form magazine which is aimed particularly at students new to post-16 courses. The magazine, 'Help Yourself', covers a range of 'helpful' topics such as services and grants for students, coping with homework, getting on with parents and so on. You have agreed to write an article for the magazine on the legal rights of students who are 16 to 17 years old. The editor has sent you a memo giving you some advice on how to write the article:

From: The Editor: 'Help Yourself'

Subject: Article: – 'You and Your Rights'

1 We'd like you to write one of two articles under the main heading, 'You and Your Rights'. The two articles will be on the topics below. As I'm giving you first choice of topic, please let me know soon which one you will be doing:

Either:

You and Your Body
Health
Sex and marriage
Drinking and smoking

Or:

Becoming Independent
Handling money
Getting a job
Driving and transport

2 Use the material attached, entitled 'You and Your Rights', which we've simplified from a leaflet by The Children's Legal Centre.

3 I'd assume that your reader is either 16 or 17 years of age. So, in writing each section, make sure you distinguish:
– their rights before they became 16;
– their rights now, at age 16 or 17;
– the rights they won't get until they're 18 or 21.
Also, could you point out the so-called 'rights' which actually depend on the final say of our parents or guardians?

4 On lay-out and presentation, please:
– use a standard article format of a title for the article, and headings for each of the three sections;
– don't forget a short introductory paragraph to outline your subject matter and get your reader's attention. Something like, 'Now you are described as "young adults" you may like to know ...';
– try to keep the article to about 500 words in length;
– include a sketch of the lay-out, indicating where you want title, headings, text and illustrations on 2 sides of A4 paper. (This will be a guide only. The editorial team may have to make some changes later.)
– write in a clear, friendly style – don't be too heavy-weight!

Thanks and good luck!

WORKING WOMEN

Woman Work

I've got the children to tend
The clothes to mend
The floor to mop
The food to shop
Then the chicken to fry
The baby to dry
I got company to feed
The garden to weed
I've got the shirts to press
The tots to dress
The cane to be cut
I gotta clean up this hut
Then see about the sick
And the cotton to pick.

Shine on me, sunshine
Rain on me, rain
Fall softly, dewdrops
And cool my brow again.

Storm, blow me from here
With your fiercest wind
Let me float across the sky
'Til I can rest again.

Fall gently, snowflakes
Cover me with white
Cold icy kisses and
Let me rest tonight.

Sun, rain, curving sky
Mountain, oceans, leaf and stone
Star shine, moon glow
You're all that I can call my own.

Maya Angelou

The Heroines

We are the terraced women
piled row upon row on the sagging, slipping hillsides of our
    lives.
We tug reluctant children up slanting streets
the pushchair wheels wedging in the ruts.
Breathless and bad-tempered we shift the Tesco carrier-bags
    from hand to hand
and stop to watch the town.

The hilltops creep away like children playing games.

Our other children shriek against the schoolyard rails –
    'There's Mandy's mum, John's mum, Dave's mum, Kate's
    mum, Ceri's mother, Tracey's mummy.'
We wave with hands scarred by groceries and too much
    washing-up
catching echoes as we pass of old wild games.

After lunch, more bread and butter, tea,
we dress in blue and white and pink and white checked
    overalls
and do the house and scrub the porch and sweep the street
and clean all the little terraces
up and down and up and down and up and down the hill.

Later, before the end-of-school bell rings,
all the babies are asleep
Mandy's mum joins Ceri's mum across the street
running to avoid the rain
and Dave's mum and John's mum – the others too – stop by
    for tea
and briefly we are wild women
girls with secrets, travellers, engineers, courtesans, and
    stars of fiction, films
plotting our escape like jail-birds
terraced, Tescoed prisoners rising from the household dust
like heroines.

Penny Windsor

My Brilliant Career

This extract is from an Australian novel, written in 1900 by Miles Franklin when she was only sixteen. She hated her existence as a member of a poor, pioneering family living in the Australian bush. When her father, a cattle rancher, goes bankrupt, her mother asks her to consider her future.

As I was getting to bed one night my mother came into my room and said seriously, 'Sybylla, I want to have a talk with you.'

'Talk away,' I responded rather sullenly, for I expected a long sing-song about my good-for-nothingness in general – a subject of which I was heartily tired.

'Sybylla, I've been studying the matter over a lot lately. It's no use, we cannot afford to keep you at home. You'll have to get something to do.'

I made no reply, and my mother continued, 'I am afraid we will have to break up the home altogether. It's no use; your father has no idea of making a living. I regret the day I ever saw him. Since he has taken to drink he has no more idea of how to make a living than a cat. I will have to give the little ones to some of the relatives; the bigger ones will have to go out to service, and so will your father and I. That's all I can see ahead of us. Poor little Gertie is too young to go out in the world (she was not twelve months younger than I); she must go to your grandmother, I think.'

I still made no reply, so my mother inquired, 'Well, Sybylla, what do you think of the matter?'

'Do you think it absolutely necessary to break up the home?' I said.

'Well, you suggest something better if you are so clever,' said mother, crossly. 'That is always the way; if I suggest a thing it is immediately put down, yet there is never any one to think of things but me. What would you do? I suppose you think you could make a living on the place for us yourself.'

'Why can't we live at home? Blackshaw and Jansen have no bigger places than we, and families just as large, and yet they make a living. It would be terrible for the little ones to grow up separated; they would be no more to each other than strangers.'

'Yes; it is all very well for you to talk like that, but how is your father to start again with only five cows in the world? It's no use, you never talk sense. You'll find my way is always the best in the end.'

'Would it not be easier,' I replied, 'for our relations to each give a little towards setting us up again, than to be burdened with the whole responsibility of rearing a child? I'm sure they'd much prefer it.'

'Yes, perhaps it would be better, but I think *you* will have to get your own living. What would they say about having to support such a big girl as you are?'

'I will go and earn my own living, and when you get me weeded out of the family you will have a perfect paradise. Having no evil to copy, the children will grow up saints,' I said bitterly.

'Now, Sybylla, it is foolish to talk like that, for you know that you take no interest in your work. If you'd turn to and help me rear poultry and make dresses – and why don't you take to cooking?'

'Take to cooking!' I retorted with scorn. 'The fire that a fellow has to endure on that old oven would kill a horse, and the grit and dirt of clearing it up grinds on my very nerves. Besides, if I ever do want to do any extra fancy cooking, we either can't afford the butter or the currants, or else the eggs are too scarce! Cook, be grannied!'

'Sybylla! Sybylla, you are getting very vulgar!'

'Yes, I once was foolish enough to try and be polite, but I've given it up. My style of talk is quite good enough for my company. What on earth does it matter whether I'm vulgar or not. I can feed calves and milk and grind out my days here just as well vulgar as unvulgar,' I answered savagely.

'There, you see you are always discontented about your home. It's no use; the only thing is for you to earn your own living.'

'I will earn my own living.'

'What will you do? Will you be examined for a pupil-teacher? That is a very nice occupation for girls.'

'What chance would I have in a competitive exam, against Goulburn girls? They all have good teachers and give up their time to study. I only have old Harris, and he is the most idiotic old animal alive; besides, I loathe the very thought of teaching. I'd as soon go on the wallaby.'*

'You are not old enough to be a general servant or a cook; you have not experience enough to be a housemaid; you don't take to sewing, and there is no chance of being accepted as a hospital nurse: you must confess there is nothing you can do. You are really a very useless girl for your age.'

'There are heaps of things I could do.'

'Tell me a few of them.'

I was silent. The professions at which I felt I had the latent power

* 'on the wallaby' : on the scrounge/ to beg.

to excel, were I but given a chance, were in a sphere far above us, and to mention my feelings and ambitions to my matter-of-fact practical mother would bring upon me worse ridicule than I was already forced to endure day by day.

'Mention a few of the things you could do.'

I might as well have named flying as the professions I was thinking of. Music was the least unmentionable of them, so I brought it forward.

'Music! But it would take years of training and great expense before you could earn anything at that! It is quite out of the question. The only thing for you to do is to settle down and take interest in your work, and help make a living at home, or else go out as a nurse-girl, and work your way up. If you have any ability in you it would soon show. If you think you could do such strokes† and the home work is not good enough for you, go out and show the world what a wonderful creature you are.'

'Mother, you are unjust and cruel!' I exclaimed. 'You do not understand me at all. I never thought I could do strokes. I cannot help being constituted so that grimy manual labour is hateful to me, for it *is* hateful to me, and I hate it more and more every day, and you can preach and preach till you go black in the face, and still I'll hate it more than ever. If I have to do it all my life, and if I'm cursed with a long life, I'll hate it just as much at the end as I do now. I'm sure it's not any wish of mine that I'm born with inclinations for better things. If I could be born again, and had the designing of myself, I'd be born the lowest and coarsest-minded person imaginable, so that I could find plenty of companionship, or I'd be born an idiot, which would be better still.'

† 'strokes' : worl as in 'different strokes for different folks'.

Miles Franklin

Woman Work
and
The Heroines

Comparison of two poems

'Woman Work' by Maya Angelou and 'The Heroines' by Penny Windsor are both about the common and often mundane aspects of women's lives. Read the two poems through carefully then answer the following questions:

1   What clues does each poem give us about where it is set?

2   What similarities in the life style of the women in each poem can you detect?

3   What are the obvious *differences* in the women's respective life styles?

4   How do the women in the two poems achieve some form of escape from the routine of their lives?

5   Both poems express a form of protest about the conditions of the women's lives. Discuss the differing ways in which the two poems convey this protest by comparing each poet's use of:
    – line length
    – sentence length and pattern
    – rhyme
    – repetition of words or phrases
    – descriptive detail
    – imagery (similes and metaphors).

6   In your view, which poem is the more successful in making its point? Why do you think this?

Creative writing

1   Write a poem which is a 'male' version of either 'The Heroines' or 'Woman Work'. For example, if you choose to use 'The Heroines' as your model, entitle your poem 'The Heroes', and imagine the lives of the men married to the women in the poem. Think of the ways in which they are also trapped by their work or unemployment and their means of escape. Try to use a similar style to the chosen poem.

2   Write a story entitled 'The Escape'. Take a character, either from one of the two poems or from 'My Brilliant Career' and write the story of how she manages to change her life, for better or for worse.

Discussion and understanding

Read the passage carefully, then discuss or write down the answers to the following questions:

1 What is Sybylla's main point of view in the argument with her mother? For instance, does she want to earn her own living or to stay at home?

2 Describe the type of work she will do if she stays at home. What appears to be her future there?

3 Various occupations are mentioned as ways in which Sybylla could earn a living. Which are they and for what reasons is each dismissed in turn by her?

4 Sybylla is unwilling to mention 'the professions at which I felt I had the latent power to excel'. What does she mean by this? How does her unwillingness to speak turn out to be justified?

5 What is Sybylla's explanation for hating her home life? Why would she prefer to have been 'born an idiot'?

6 Do you think her situation would have been any easier as a boy?

Oral work

1 Form pairs: one of you take the role of a parent and the other, a son or daughter. Improvise a scene in which the two have an argument about the young person's future. Bring out the differences in the expectations between the two.

   For example, a father may want his son to take science subjects at college in order to get 'a decent job', but the son has other ideas.

2 In pairs, one of you take the role of Sybylla's mother, and the other a *son* in Sybylla's position. Suppose the son is a restless, ambitious person like Sybylla. Work out a scene in which an argument develops about *his* future. Bring out the differences in the expectations you imagine both mother and son would have about his future life.

Creative writing

Develop one of the role-play subjects above into a written dialogue, either as a short story or as an extract from a novel. (See *Techniques*: 'Writing dialogue'.)

Writing dialogue

This section helps you to understand the importance of dialogue in imaginative writing and fiction, as well as to use dialogue in your own writing. The exercises here are linked with the passage from 'My Brilliant Career'.

Why use dialogue?

Dialogue, or conversation, between two or more characters, can be a very important technique in your imaginative writing. Here are three of the main reasons why:

1 Plot

Rather than depending solely on the narrative for revealing new plot information, you can use a character as a 'mouthpiece'. This can often be a more dramatic and powerful means of telling something than relying on the narrator.

In 'My Brilliant Career', Sybylla as narrator tells us of the family's debts caused by a severe drought and her father's weakness for drink. But it is from the dialogue that we learn of the mother's plan to break up the home.

- Why might it be more effective to learn of this fact in the dialogue, rather than in the narrative?

2 Character

If you are writing about more than one character, dialogue is a valuable means of portraying a whole spectrum of features about a person:

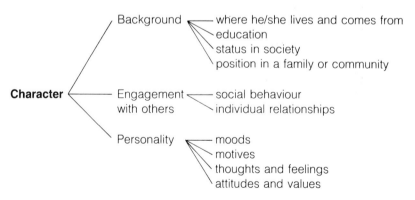

Character
— Background — where he/she lives and comes from
  education
  status in society
  position in a family or community
— Engagement with others — social behaviour
  individual relationships
— Personality — moods
  motives
  thoughts and feelings
  attitudes and values

- Taking each point on the right hand side of the chart in turn, what do you learn of Sybylla's character, both from *what* she says and *the way* she says it?

It is unlikely that in a short piece of imaginative writing, you could portray such a spectrum of characteristics – you will be selective according to the purpose of the writing. For example, you may quite deliberately want to give a limited view of a character – stressing only one or two features. Say one character in your dialogue is an 'upper-class twit'. It may be sufficient to characterise this figure of fun by giving him a posh accent and a snobbish attitude to life.

3 Theme

If you wish to put forward certain views, ideas or themes in your writing, you can use a character as a mouthpiece for these. For example, you might use a conversation between a master of the hounds and an anti-hunt protester to debate your views on bloodsports. But in a story, your dialogues will become tedious if you are using them merely to present points of view. A story should have a *number* of intentions – lively plot, interesting characters, thought-provoking themes and good use of language.

- Can you identify any important themes in the passage from 'My Brilliant Career' which may be developed through the novel?

Tips on writing dialogue

1 Make it dynamic

Try to write dialogue in a lively, vigorous way. Obviously what you write must be appropriate to the subject. For example, a dialogue between a mother and her son whom she is visiting for the first time in prison is unlikely to be a cheerful repartee, but you *can* convey energy and emotion in what they say. Try to avoid using lengthy speeches in a dialogue and make sure that your characters react to each other.

2 Make it sound natural

While dialogue in imaginative writing is bound to be more heightened than conversation in life, try to write it as real people speak – give the characters real things to say. Sometimes it helps to model a character's way of speaking on someone you know, or on conversations you have heard. The test of a good dialogue is whether it works when it is read aloud; so try this!

3   ## Give it a purpose

You need to plan beforehand what you want the dialogue to achieve. Do you wish to: further the plot, portray character, explore an idea, or simply get a response from your reader such as laughter or shock? You may not be able to achieve all these purposes, but a well-written dialogue will often accomplish more than one of them.

4   Make it true to character

If you are using stereotyped characters, like the upper-class twit or a gossiping housewife, it is not too difficult to make them true to type by using appropriate speech mannerisms such as a dialect, a repeated phrase, a characteristic expression or a speech defect.

If you are using realistic characters, you will need to think how you can use their speech to portray the distinctive features which make them individuals. To help you, look at the passage from 'My Brilliant Career'.

- What do you find distinctive about the *way* Sybylla speaks which seems to reflect her character?

EQUAL OPPORTUNITIES

The Equal Pay Act 1970

Under The Equal Pay Act 1970, it is unlawful to pay a woman less than a man for doing the same or broadly similar work, or work that has been rated as of the same value as a man's, under a job evaluation scheme. If a shop pays its female assistants less than its male assistants for doing exactly the same job, or doing a very similar job, it is breaking the law. If it offers men promotion opportunities where they can earn more money, but does not offer these to women, it might be breaking both The Equal Pay Act and The Sex Discrimination Act.

These laws forbid discrimination against men as well as women.

The police don't have any power to operate these laws, however. The Equal Opportunities Commission can investigate and take action, but mostly individuals themselves have to complain to an industrial tribunal, or the Secretary of State for Education, or the county courts.

Since 1973 Britain has belonged to the European Economic Community (EEC). The EEC has the power to make laws, and has legislated equal pay for equal work. Some people, who have not been able to get equal pay under our Equal Pay Act, have gone to the European Court of Justice (which can make decisions which this country has to follow), and have been successful in their applications.

Julie Hayward, a cook at a Merseyside shipyard. She made legal history when she won her case to receive the same pay as men whose jobs were different but were considered to be of equal value.

The Sex Discrimination Act 1975

Since 1975 it has been against the law to discriminate on grounds of sex in:
- employment and training
- education
- housing
- the provision of goods, facilities and services.

So if a firm turns down a woman who is well-qualified for a job in favour of a man who is not so well-qualified, the firm may be acting unlawfully. This is **direct discrimination.**

If a firm requires all its employees to be over a certain height (which most women would not reach), the firm may be acting unlawfully. This is **indirect discrimination.**

However, there are many exemptions and exceptions to The Sex Discrimination Act. The Act does not apply in the following cases.

Work
- If you work, or apply to work, for a firm which employs fewer than six people
- If you attend a single-sex school or college
- If you belong to, or want to join, one of the Armed Forces
- If you work in a private household
- If you apply to work for a church (some churches will not ordain women)
- If you work all or most of the time outside Great Britain
- If you are male and want to work as a midwife (only a limited number are accepted)
- If you are female and want to work in a mine
- If there is a genuine need for someone of a particular sex do the job (for example, an actor)

Housing
- If you try to rent accommodation in a house that the owner lives in or shares

Welfare services
- If you belong to a voluntary organisation or a charity whose main purpose is to provide benefits for one sex only (for example, Boys' Clubs)
- If you need special care, supervision or attention in a hospital, prison, hostel, or old people's home

Rights, Responsibilities and the Law
by Judith Edmunds

BILL ODDIE

I READ a really interesting article last week, but the baby ate it. I can remember roughly what it said though. Apparently, scientists have, once and for all, irrefutably proved that men and women are different. Oh, you knew that?

No, what I mean is ... you know different sections of the human brain control different abilities and faculties. Well, by using some kind of cranial camera (they stick the lens in your ear I suppose), scientists have observed that men and women's brains develop in different ways. Unfortunately I can't remember exactly what ways.

I know the general conclusion was that men can't help being good at physically violent activities, and maths (which explains why men are better at boxing ... they can hit one another AND count each other out). Whilst women really are better suited to cooking, and operating computers. That's a bit of a simplification but it was something like that.

The point is it means many of the differences between the sexes are natural and not all the result of historical conditioning and biased education. This shouldn't come as much of a surprise. After all, let's own up, basically we are animals (mammals, no less) and in the animal kingdom the role of the sexes is generally pretty consistent.

Take birds. The males tend to wear silly coloured feathers and prance around showing off to the females, or else they're fighting other males; whilst the females usually get on with laying the eggs and bringing up the chicks.

I'll happily accept that men and women are much like the birds but which is "better"? (Men or women, I mean). Well, I reckon bringing up kids is a slightly more constructive activity than belting one another. Surely mankind measures his (or her) civilisation by how far we've come since our primitive start in the jungle?

It seems to me that by any logic the more civilised we get the more women should play leading roles in our society. Does this happen? Also ... consider this: how many women football hooligans do you know? Or muggers? Or burglars? Or rapists? Or drug pushers? Or ... or ... or ... (fill in the blanks and then go on to the next question).

The Guardian 5 Nov 1986

Science for Girls

At the age of about 13, girls have to decide which subjects to concentrate on at school, and which to drop.

It's one of the most vital decisions they'll ever make. Because, quite literally, it will affect the rest of their lives.

Yet for various reasons, far too many of them get it wrong. Because of lack of serious thought, outdated ideas about the lives they'll lead, a wish to be just like their friends or the absence of informed advice from parents, they are quite likely to avoid the subjects that will be of most real use to them.

Today, the opportunities are there…

Yet, nowadays, the education system offers girls a better chance than ever before. Since the Sex Discrimination Act of 1975, schools must provide subjects and facilities equally for both sexes.

So all the subjects available to boys, and which serve them so well in later life, must also be there for girls. Now, it's up to the girls themselves, and their parents, to make sure that they benefit fully from these opportunities.

…and girls CAN do it.

Despite the opportunities offered, the majority of girls still continue to avoid certain subjects, largely in the mistaken belief that they're not "girls' subjects." These include maths, the physical sciences and technical subjects.

But there's absolutely no reason for this belief. At primary school girls are better than boys at arithmetic. Girls in single-sex schools are as good as anybody at science and maths. Where girls take technical subjects, they prove very able and enjoy them immensely.

Why it's important.

Today, more than ever, there are very good reasons why all girls should, at the very least, seriously consider taking these subjects.

Because, despite what anyone says, these are the ones they'll need to live and work in the modern world. Even the patronising old argument that "girls only

They're all happy with their choice!

A trained electrician, Karyl Keenan works at the famous Vickers Shipbuilding and Engineering works in Barrow-in-Furness. The photograph shows her carrying out the kind of highly skilled job that is part of her normal working day – in this case connecting up a multi-core, low-power junction box, on board a ship being built in the yard.

Photo: Courtesy of Vickers Shipbuilding & Engineering Ltd

Angela Hull achieved a distinction in her City & Guilds course at the Building Crafts Training School in London and now works as a stonemason for a firm of architectural craftsmen. She began stone carving as a hobby and previously restored pottery before taking her TOPS course.

Her skill so impressed the master mason she works with that she was given the job of restoring the figures of Christ over the north transept door of Westminster Abbey.

Photo: Bill Mackenzie, London

Sheila Edmundson was the first woman to get a foreign-going Master's Certificate in the Merchant Navy and is a second officer with Ellerman Lines, spending alternate months at sea and at home. "I like being at sea," she says, "because you have to pit your wits against the elements."

She studied at Portsmouth Technical College and joined the merchant navy as a cadet. A recent survey proves that the U.K. leads the world in the number of female Merchant Navy officers with a total of 255.

Photo: Courtesy of Ellerman Lines.

Job areas requiring or preferring science/maths qualifications:

Agriculture
Air Traffic Control
Animals – work with
Archaeology
Architecture
Astronomy
Aviation
Bacteriology
Beauty Therapy
Biochemistry
Biology
Botany
Building
Cartography
Catering
Chemistry
Chiropody
Dentistry
Design
Dietetics
Engineering
Environmental Health
Factory Inspectorate
Fish Farming
Floristry
Food Science
Forensic Science
Forestry
Geology
Hairdressing
Home Economics
Horticulture

Laboratory Work
Landscape Architecture
Marine Biology
Medical Laboratory
Sciences
Medicine
Meteorology
Microbiology
Midwifery
Nursing
Nutrition
Oceanography
Occupational Therapy
Optical Work
Patent Work
Pharmacology
Pharmacy
Photography
Printing
Psychology
Physics
Physiotherapy
Radiography
Remedial Gymnastics
Speech Therapy
Surveying
Teaching
Technician
Trichology
Veterinary Science
Zoology

get married" is no longer true, if it ever was. More women continue to work and return to work after marriage than ever before. Indeed, two thirds of the working women in this country are also married.

So these are the subjects most likely to avoid a dead-end job or a place on the dole queue. They're also the ones most likely now to lead to college, a satisfying, well-paid career and the confidence to deal with an increasingly technological world.

Jobs for the girls.

As the list here shows, a surprising number of job areas today require or at least prefer some knowledge of maths and science. On top of that, traditional "women's" jobs are in decline and available vacancies increasingly call for some technical know-how.

In fact, this is where the future lies. Britain is going to be short of technicians and skilled people. It's a field in which girls can do very well and the Engineering Industry Training Board is keen to help them, with practical help and careers advice.

Pennie Bellas is the station master in charge of Burgess Hill and Hassocks stations, on British Rail's southern region. She has an honours degree in industrial relations and economics and is in charge of station staff, deals with emergencies, signal faults, points failures, fires and accidents, should they occur.

She says, 'I'm ready to get out on the line dealing with points or uncoupling the train – there are lots of opportunities for me to progress up the BR ladder.'

Photo: Courtesy of Syndication International Ltd.

Diane Lewis works on a drilling machine as part of her training on a Youth Opportunities Programme course organised by the Manchester YMCA's 'Training for Life' scheme. The course which includes instruction in basic skills, project work and integrated schemes, is attended by day-release and residential trainees.

Photo: Courtesy of YMCA, Manchester.

After leaving school at 17, Zandra Bradley joined H.M. Dockyard, Chatham as an apprentice electrical fitter and through day release and evening classes gained her City & Guilds certificate in engineering and then an ONC in engineering, followed by HNC certificates.

Now 24, Zandra works in the Dockyard's Nuclear Submarine Division as an assistant electrical test officer, inspecting, testing and putting into operation electronic and electro-mechanical systems.

Photo: Courtesy of Department of Industry.

Subject Options at School
by the Equal Opportunities Commission

The first three activities are oral work. These have been designed so that a small group of students in the class can select one particular topic of interest to them and work together on it. The work for the Survey could be shared between two groups.

Each activity here, whether oral or written, requires you to read all three pieces of reading material: that is, the Equality Acts, Bill Oddie's article and the leaflet on 'Science for Girls'.

Survey

1 Read the 'Science for Girls' leaflet carefully, then conduct a class survey to find out whether preferences according to sex can be detected in girls' and boys' choice of subjects and intended career direction. Perhaps break down the line of inquiry and select *two* of the following areas:
   – subjects dropped at about age 13
   – subjects/courses being studied now
   – intentions for the future
       e.g. further study: which subjects?
       training courses: which occupation?
   – reasons for: girls dropping Science subjects;
                    boys dropping Arts/Languages.

2 In your group, decide on the best way to tabulate your findings so that:
   – the distinction between girls' and boys' choices is clear;
   – the categorising of subjects/courses is meaningful.
       e.g. Is a simple division between Arts and Sciences precise enough for you to record all the courses students in your class are now following? Or will you need other categories?

3 Then analyse your findings so that you can draw conclusions about preferences according to sex (if they exist) in subject and career choices.
       e.g. 'The results show that almost twice as many boys as girls in the class now study Science subjects.'

4 Present your findings to the class.

Debating speeches

1 In pairs, select *one or more* of the professions below. In each case, decide between you who will make the speech in defence of that sex in the selected profession and who will make the speech attacking it:

Male midwife	Female TV sports commentator
Male secretary/typist	Female rugby player
Male nanny/au pair	Female lorry driver
Male beautician	Female combat soldier
Male infant-school teacher	Female welder

2   Preferably carry out some research for your speech, so that you know what you are talking about. You might look in the Careers section in your library and/or talk to a Careers teacher. Then write a short and persuasive speech.

3   In your pair, present your speeches for and against the selected profession(s) to the class. They can then vote on the speech they found most persuasive.

Radio commercial

1   In a small group, use the 'Sciences for Girls' leaflet to write a 30-second radio commercial, made by the Equal Opportunities Commission. The aim is to persuade girls of thirteen years of age, choosing their subject options for exams, to pursue Science, Mathematics and Technology.
(See Case-study, chapter 4 for writing a radio script for a commercial.)

2   In choosing your material and writing the commentary, consider carefully the age and wide ability range of your 13-year-old audience. How will you make your points clear, appealing and forceful?

3   When you have worked out a script, which may use such effects as music, a voice-over, sound effects and comments from girls in science jobs, prepare to rehearse it for tape-recording.

4   Once the tape is completed, play it back to your class, or even better, to a 13-year-old audience for their opinion!

Writing

1   'Despite the Acts for Equal Pay and against Sex Discrimination, it is still true to say that some jobs are more suitable for men and others more suitable for women.' Discuss.

2   'Men can't help being physically violent . . . whilst women really are better suited to cooking . . .' (*See Bill Oddie*'s article). Argue either for or against this view.
(For help on an argument essay, see *Techniques*: 'Drafting an argument essay', chapter 8.)

3   Despite much publicity aimed at encouraging girls to opt for Science and Technology careers, they are still not doing so. Discuss the possible reasons for this and what, if anything, can be done about it.

8

LIVING TO TELL THE TALE

CAR ACCIDENT

Meditation on the A30

A man on his own in a car
   Is revenging himself on his wife:
He opens the throttle and bubbles with dottle
   And puffs at his pitiful life:

She's losing her looks very fast.
   She loses her temper all day;
That lorry won't let me get past.
   This Mini is blocking my way.

Why can't you step on it and shift her!
   I can't go on crawling like this!
At breakfast she said that she wished I was dead –
   Thank heavens we don't have to kiss.

I'd like a nice blonde on my knee
   And one who won't argue or nag.
Who dares to come hooting at *me*?
   I only give way to a Jag.

You're barmy or plastered, I'll pass you, you bastard –
   I *will* overtake you. I *will*!
As he clenches his pipe, his moment is ripe
   And the corner's accepting its kill.

John Betjeman

The Fallen Birdman

The oldman in the cripplechair
Died in transit through the air
And slopped into the road.

The driver of the lethal lorry
Trembled out and cried: 'I'm sorry,
But it was his own fault.'

Humans snuggled round the mess
In masochistic tenderness
As raindrops danced in his womb.

But something else obsessed my brain.
The canvas, twisted steel and cane,
His chair spreadeagled in the rain.
Like a fallen birdman.

Roger McGough

The Crash

Trevor is not a reckless driver. In fact sixty miles per hour on the M5 Motorway is the fastest he ever goes. He doesn't rush and he never gets annoyed; he likes to stay relaxed and to take things easily. As he drives, he listens to Gregorian chants because they help him to relax. He has been driving for eight years and has only had one accident and that was a bump in the Sainsbury's car park.

Little does Trevor know, whilst driving along in his totally relaxed manner, that in just nine minutes' time his car will meet with the central crash barrier and catapult him thirty feet into the air, causing the total destruction of six people. He can't feel the pain that will shoot through his body in his last dying seconds. He knows little of the car, coming in the opposite direction, on which he will land, causing grief and despair to friends and relations. He is totally unaware of what is going to happen. All he thinks of is keeping on the road and driving safely. His final minutes tick away on his clock that will stop when all the agony in the world will shoot through his limbs.

Just one and a half minutes to go, and, totally unaware, Trevor pulls out to overtake a big lorry which has moved into the centre lane. He moves out into the third lane, raises his speed to just above sixty miles per hour, and begins to overtake. He thinks nothing of the fact that his six-year-old car doesn't have special tyres or suspension. He is only going slightly faster than the lorry and it takes quite a long time to pass. The second hand has five seconds to go. It ticks away to zero. Trevor's brain won't register anything again; it all happens far too quickly.

The front tyre blows and the car swerves violently towards the central barrier, throwing Trevor about in his seat. The car is doing just over sixty miles per hour and it meets violently and decisively with the barrier. The right-hand front wing concertinas and the chassis shakes like an erupting volcano. The vibrations shoot through Trevor's body. The rear end of the car sails into the air, pulling the rest of the chassis with it. The car elegantly twists and rolls like a gymnast, reaches its peak and begins its descent, still rolling and twisting. The car gains speed and thunders through the roof of a family saloon on its way to the beach. All five people inside are killed.

The chassis of Trevor's car crumples as it meets with the saloon and Trevor's head meets with the steering wheel. The man who took nine months to create and three hours to deliver, is devastated in just 2.3 seconds.

Ashley Cook (a student)

This could happen to you

use a crossing-it's up to 5 times safer

 Issued by the Department of the Environment, the Scottish Development Department and the Welsh Office.

Printed in England for Her Majesty's Stationery Office by Impress Artpak Ltd, London. Dd 123358 8 73

Read this and ease off on the accelerator this weekend

A MAN WAS KILLED

EVERY YEAR on the roads of this country there are 260,000 accidents in which 7,000 people are killed, 340,000 injured. This is the story of one of those accidents. One man died, another was badly hurt. I followed the police as they sorted out the facts. Then, when their file was closed with a verdict of "dangerous driving", I back-tracked on the case. I wanted to discover every factor which had turned this particular incident into tragedy.

by DENIS HOLMES

The accident happened at 10.03 p.m. At county police headquarters an accident file was opened. The first entry tells the whole story – and none of it.

"SALOON motor-car, 1,500 c.c., overtakes estate car and collides head-on with solo motor-cycle, 650 cc. Rider of motor-cycle suffered multiple fractures to head. Other injuries to chest and legs. Fatal.

"Driver of motor-car suffered concussion. Cuts to face and head. Blinded in right eye from windscreen glass. Serious.

"Weather fine, road dry, dark, no moon. No road sign in vicinity. No speed limits or other restrictions in operation. Road conditions not a contributory factor."

the POLICE said:

A patrol car arrived at the scene of the crash at 10.30. The constable who made the first inquiries made his report:

"I WAS told that there were a car and a motor-cycle involved and that one injured man was sitting in a car while another was lying beside the road on the grass.

"I first located the man lying beside the road. He was wearing motor-cycling clothes. He had sustained severe head injuries and apart from other injuries it was obvious that he was dead. I did not touch the body at this stage.

"I moved on farther along the road to locate the injured man. I could see he had serious injuries to his head and face. He seemed unable to see. The blood and injuries appeared to be worse in the vicinity of his right eye. There was a great deal of glass around his eyes.

"I said to him: 'I am a police officer. Can you hear what I am saying?' He nodded and I then asked: 'Can you see anything?'

"He replied: 'No, nothing at all.' I asked him how I could contact his family and he replied: 'I was going home. My wife is not well. Do not worry her.'"

the AMBULANCE MAN said:

The ambulance driver who went to the crash reported in his duty log:

"THE motor-cyclist had multiple injuries to his head and I found life extinct. He was wearing a black leather jacket, blue denim trousers, a left riding boot and a left-hand gauntlet-type glove. His clothing was torn. He was not wearing a crash helmet."

the WITNESS said:

There were two witnesses to the accident. The first was the driver of the estate car which was overtaken by the crash saloon. His statement:

" I WAS driving home with my wife. The weather was good, the road dry, and the visibility excellent.

"I was travelling at about 45 m.p.h. I was on the brow of the hill when I saw the single light of a motor-cycle coming towards me. Behind it were the lights of another vehicle.

"I could not say how far away these lights were, but they were not a great distance and I could see from their angle that they were starting to climb the hill. I dipped my headlights and eased my speed slightly.

"Then I saw lights in my mirror and realised that a vehicle was moving up behind me. Suddenly I realised that this vehicle behind had pulled out to overtake me. It did this just as the motor-cycle had drawn level with my bonnet from the opposite direction.

"They hit each other right beside me. They were so close that flying glass from the crash hit my car and my wife screamed. I stopped farther along at the side of the road.

"As I got out I saw that the car which had overtaken me had run on for a fair way and then disappeared off the side of the road.

"I found the driver lying in the driving seat. He did not seem able to see but was alive. I asked him if there was anyone with him who might be trapped and he shook his head.

"I then ran back to find the motor-cyclist. I didn't touch him but he looked in a very bad way.

"I just cannot understand why the car driver tried to get past me at this point. He could not have seen over the brow of the hill as I could but he should have seen the lights of the approaching vehicles.

"If only he had waited until he was over the brow he would have found a straight road for a quarter of a mile where he could have overtaken me easily."

the DRIVER said:

The driver of the car which was following the motor-cyclist corroborated this very full description. He stated:

" I WAS driving at about 50 m.p.h. behind a motor-cycle which had overtaken me some time back. The motor-cycle was being driven perfectly correctly but was pulling away from me up the slope of the hill.

"I saw the lights of a vehicle approaching from the opposite direction and as it came over the brow of the hill towards me its lights dipped down.

"Suddenly the undipped lights of another vehicle showed up and pulled out from behind the first one. It came straight at us on our side of the road. I could see the motor-cyclist outlined in the glare. There was a bang like a bomb going off and a crash of breaking glass.

"The motor-cycle vanished and the lights of the other vehicle came charging at me, still on my side of the road and went off the road to my right.

"I stopped and ran over to the car. I found the driver slumped in the front seat. The windscreen was broken and it looked as if his head had gone through it. I asked him if he was all right. He couldn't speak very well, but I heard him say: 'Help me, I am blind. I am blind.'

"Another man who came along went to get help while I stayed with the injured man.

"The car driver just couldn't have seen if it was clear to overtake before he pulled out."

the INJURED MAN said:

The injured motorist, a 27-year-old businessman who had no previous accidents or motoring convictions in five years of driving, suffered a complete loss of memory of the moments immediately before the crash. All he could tell of the accident was:

" I HAD been driving home after making business calls. I had been worried about money matters and because my wife was unwell. The doctor did not seem able to find out what was wrong with her.

"I had been driving for some time and was nearly home when I stopped for a drink and a sandwich. I do not drink much normally and I did not have much that night. I certainly was not drunk. Neither did I go excessively fast.

"I remember coming up behind a car going in the same direction as myself. Everything seemed normal although it appeared to be going rather slowly. I could not believe that it was me who hit the motor-cycle."

the ENGINEERS said:

The two vehicles involved in the accident were both examined carefully by engineers.

The motor-cycle appeared to have been in perfect condition.

Examination of the badly damaged car revealed that the off-side front wheel was buckled and the tyre on it had burst. Tyre pressures on the other three wheels were all different and incorrect. All the tyres were badly worn.

As with the motor-cycle, the damage was too extensive to enable a road test to be made.

The motor-cyclist's father was traced and he stated:

"MY boy was 21. He was perfectly fit and had good eye-sight and hearing.

"He had been riding motor cycles for four years and had plenty of experience in all weathers. He had never had an accident of any kind. He normally wore a crash helmet.

"He had no alcohol to drink that evening and as far as I know had no intention of going anywhere for a drink. His motorcycle was in good condition and he took pride in keeping it clean and in good order."

The crash helmet was found later in the boy's bedroom.

and the
SENTENCE was:

The motorist was charged with dangerous driving and sentenced to a heavy fine and a long period of disqualification. The file was closed.

"THE crime and punishment part was over. Now the police and I back-tracked on the case.

We knew exactly *what* had happened. Our job now was to discover the *why* and the *how*, to isolate the factors which led to the accident.

Our aim was to see if we could learn anything which might prevent future accidents or reduce their severity.

FACTOR ONE: The motorcyclist was not wearing a crash helmet. Obviously this could not affect the car driver's actions at all and it cannot be said positively that a helmet would have saved the motor-cyclist's life.

But a helmet would have greatly increased his chances of survival.

FACTOR TWO: Was drink a cause? The barman at the pub where the car driver stopped stated that he had half a pint of bitter with a ham sandwich. He then had two single whiskies.

Hardly enought to be significant. A medical specialist was called in for his expert view:

"The motorist was of a naturally nervous disposition and on this night he was both tired and worried. In this state two whiskies could well have impaired his safe driving abilities.

"Their effect on a man of his temperament would be to give him extra confidence while at the same time reducing his sense of driving judgment.

"Without those whiskies he might have been less impatient to overtake and might not·have misjudged the speeds."

The Chief Constable told me: "This was clearly not a case in which the prosecution could use drink as part of the charge.

"But all police and safety experts know that drink plays a bigger part in road accdents than can ever be disclosed. It is estimated that in about 18 p.c. of fatal accidents someone involved has been drinking. We believe that it would be a much larger proportion if all the background facts were known."

FACTOR THREE: The part played by speed. Although neither vehicle was going excessively fast (car about 50 m.p.h.; motor-cycle abut 55 m.p.h.) the *closing* speed was not less than 105 m.p.h.

This means that at the moment of emergency, in order to take avoiding action, the car driver would have needed the hair-trigger reactions of a Fangio.

FACTOR FOUR: The motorist was not wearing a safety belt. He was fortunate not to have been impaled on the steering column. In the event, he was thrown forward over the steering wheel and his head hit the windscreen. Both would have been averted by a belt.

FACTOR FIVE: Lack of judgment, negligence and irresponsibility. This was the only factor which figured in the prosecution against the motorist. On this he was charged with causing death by dangerous driving.

On the fatal evening he committed four clear breaches of the Highway Code:

Sect. 33: Never overtake unless you know that you can do so without danger to yourself or others.

Sect. 36: Do not overtake at or when approaching the brow of a hill.

Sect. 40: At night always drive well within the limits of your lights. (The motorist's vision was severely restricted at the point of the crash because his lights were pointing upwards as he breasted the brow of the hill).

Sect. 86: When driving behind another vehicle, dip your head-lights.

FACTOR SIX: Lack of maintenance. It is not possible to say whether the tyre burst on impact or before. But clearly the motorist had not checked the condition of his tyres lately and obviously he had not checked his tyre pressures every week.

It is quite possible that the motorist swerved at the moment of crisis and the extra strain caused the tyre to burst. If so his negligence destroyed the one chance of preventing the accident.

In this simple accident, then, there were six possible accident factors. Multiply them by the 260,000 accidents a year and you can easily see that here is scope for an attack on bad driving.

If we could only go into every accident with the same thoroughness as a murder hunt we should surely get some valuable pointers on how to cut the road toll. It could be done with enough money and manpower.

The police would still get their man. But the basic purpose of their investigations would be prevention rather than punishment.

And that's the way it should be.

Daily Mail

'It was an accident ...'

Consider these attempts by motorists to describe to their insurance companies what went wrong:

- A pedestrian hit me and went under my car.

- I collided with a stationary truck coming the other way.

- I had to run into the other car to avoid a collision.

- The guy was all over the road. I had to swerve a number of times before I hit him.

- In my attempt to kill a fly, I drove into a telegraph pole.

- The lamp-post was approaching fast. I was attempting to swerve out of its path when it struck my front end.

- An invisible car came out of nowhere, struck my vehicle and vanished.

- I knocked down an old man who said it was his fault because he had been knocked down before.

- A bull gored my car.

- I put my head out of the window but it broke because it was shut.

- I was on my way to the doctor's with rear end trouble, when my universal joint gave way, causing me to have an accident.

Motor vehicle claim form

(*Sections* a, b *and* c *have been simplified.*)

Policy no:

I authorise the Company to instruct my repairers on my behalf to undertake such repairs to my vehicle as may be agreed:

Date:_____ Signature:_____

a) Insured:

Name:_____ Occupation:_____

Address:_____

_____Telephone:_____

b) Driver:

Name:_____ Occupation:_____

Address:_____

_____ Telephone:_____

Date of birth:_____Driving licence no:_____

Date when driver passed test:_____

Details of all police convictions in connection with a motor vehicle:

_____

_____

c) Vehicle:

Make:_____

Registration no:_____cc:_____

For what purpose was vehicle being used?_____

State exact damage to the vehicle:_____

_____

_____

NOTE: an estimate of repairs must be sent as soon as possible, if the damage is to be covered by the insurance policy.

d) Accident:

Town:_____

Date:_____ Time:_____ am/pm Place:_____

Own speed:_____ Width of road:_____ Road and weather conditions:_____

_____

Was accident reported to the police?_____

Details of Officer or Station:_____

e) Other parties involved: (Give details of all persons in your vehicle who were involved in the accident or sustained injury or damage to property. Attach extra sheet if necesary.)

Name and Address	Make of vehicle, Registration and Insurer.	Details of Injury and Damage

f) Witnesses:

Names & Addresses of all passengers in your vehicle	Names & Addresses of any other witnesses

g) Full description of accident: (including details of warnings and signals given by all parties)

_____

_____

_____

_____

h) Sketch plan of accident: (Please show the position on the road of vehicles at point of impact and indicate direction and track immediately before accident. If possible, please indicate road signs and markings, including pedestrian crossings, relative importance of roads, and direction of nearest towns.)

NOTE: Any correspondence or Notices of Prosecution or other proceedings must be forwarded immediately.

I/We declare that these particulars are true and complete. I/We understand that the information given on this form may be submitted to solicitors for use in connection with any litigation arising out of this accident.

I/We authorise the Company to instruct my/our repairers on my/our behalf to undertake such repairs to my/our vehicle as may be agreed.

Signature of Insured _____ Date _____

Group oral work

The objective of this activity is to work in groups to make a tape-recording which describes an accident from the point of view of the people involved. Before you start the work below, read the poems, short story, and the Case-study material. You will also find it useful to have available copies of the Motor Vehicle Claim Form, such as the one reproduced here.

1 In groups of about four, work out the circumstances of a possible car accident. For this, either draw on actual experience – an accident which involved one of you or an accident which was reported in the news. Or, choose a fictitious situation – perhaps selecting one of the accidents described in the poems and the short story.

2 Work out the identities of the main participants in the accident – the drivers, the passengers, pedestrians involved and so on. Then allocate a role to each member of your group. For example, people in your group might choose the following roles:
   – one is the driver who causes the accident
   – one is a passenger in a car whose driver is killed
   – one is a pedestrian who is almost hit
   – one is a police officer who arrives on the scene later.

3 As a group, fill out a copy of the Claim Form, for each driver involved in the accident. In this way, you will be able to work out the details of the accident – the timing, the location, how it happened, who was involved and so on – from one or more points of view.

4 Now on your own, make notes on the accident from the point of view of the character you have chosen. You will be using the notes for a spoken account of what happened and why.

   Think through in more detail the kind of person you are – your age, sex, background, personality and reason for being at the scene of the accident. Work out your character's point of view on the accident – for example, how much responsibility he or she feels, or is prepared to admit to. You may decide to give a controversial account!

5 Make a group tape-recording in which:
   – one of you starts by giving a brief, factual account of the accident, as may appear on a police file. (See the example in the first section of the *Daily Mail* article.)
   – each of you in turn tells your version of the accident.

6 Play the tape-recording back to the class. Let the class judge whose account is to be most trusted and who is ultimately to blame for the accident.

For the following Case-study, please read and study closely the Daily Mail *article, 'A Man Was Killed' by Denis Holmes. You may also find some inspiration from reading the poems and short story before it. The Case-study is designed mainly for individual work.*

You are a trainee reporter working for a local newspaper and have been assigned to work on a report of a fatal car accident involving local people, which your editor has indicated is 'front page material'. You were unable to reach the site of the car accident, which caused the death of a local youth and severe injury to a local business man. However, you have been able to obtain copies of a number of statements from an accident file at county police headquarters. These statements are from the police, two witnesses and the injured man. (See 'A Man Was Killed'.)

As in any local newspaper report, your editor is concerned that you stress the ways in which this event affects local people and their concerns. As part of your training, he has asked you to write *two* versions of this report, each stressing a different local 'angle'. He will then make an editorial decision as to which version he prefers. You have been asked to choose two of the following 'angles':
- tragic loss of the life of a 21-year-old local man
- local business man's personal problems cause tragedy
- irresponsibility of business man: drinking and driving; flouting safety rules; driving a dangerous car
- local roads, poor signs, accident black-spots.

1 Rough drafts

Prepare and write the rough drafts for the two versions of the newspaper report. You have been given the following guidelines:
- the text of each draft is to be between 300 and 400 words long;
- there must be a balance between 'giving the facts' and supporting the report's point of view by using evidence (such as quotations from people involved) appropriately.

2 Editorial decision

When you have finished the two drafts, ask either another member of your class or your teacher to be 'editor', and to select the version which seems the more promising as front page material of a local newspaper. Ask this 'editor' to justify his or her choice, which you must then accept!

3 Writing the report

In finishing your report, you have two further jobs to do:
- design a rough lay-out of the report as it will appear on the front page, including headline, space for a picture, a caption underneath this and columns for the text;
- finally design and write up (or type) your final version, making it read and look like a real newspaper front page report.

THE NUCLEAR WEAPONS DEBATE

The view of the Campaign for Nuclear Disarmament:

Seven Deadly Myths About Nuclear Weapons

Nobody *likes* nuclear weapons. We all know that to use them would probably mean the end of civilisation. But many of the things people believe about why we should keep nuclear weapons are, in fact, myths. Myths like these:

1 'The Bomb has kept the peace in Europe for 40 years'

That's just a guess. Nobody knows what would have happened if nuclear weapons hadn't been invented.

But one thing is certain. No arms race has ever prevented war – only made it more terrible when it came.

Today the build-up of nuclear weapons on both sides of Europe makes war more likely, not less. It also stops us finding peaceful solutions to the problems of our divided continent.

Outside Europe there have been dozens of wars since 1945, killing millions of people. The Bomb hasn't stopped *these* wars, even though many involved countries with their own nuclear weapons.

2 'Nuclear weapons are so terrible they will never be used'

No sane person would ever start a nuclear war. But nothing human is proof against error.

With defence policies based on nuclear weapons we are gambling with life on earth. To make the nuclear threat 'credible' both sides are preparing to fight nuclear wars. NATO even says it is ready to *start* a nuclear war.

It is mad to take these risks. How can we be sure nuclear weapons will never be used? Or that the computers which control the missiles will never break down?

And with nuclear deterrence you can only fail once.

3 'You can't disinvent the Bomb'

That's true. But just because we *could* destroy the planet, doesn't mean we *have* to.

There's still time to stop the spread of nuclear weapons. But it's the nuclear nations that must start to disarm. Otherwise more and more countries will get the Bomb and sooner or later a nuclear war will be fought.

Independent action by Britain would be a great step forward on the road to disarmament. We could begin to heal the Cold War division of the world into two hostile blocs.

4 'Nuclear disarmament would leave us open to "blackmail"'

No country has ever used nuclear blackmail against a non-nuclear country.

Having the Bomb didn't help the US in Viêtnam. It hasn't helped the Russians in Afghanistan. And Britain's Polaris didn't stop Argentina from invading the Falklands.

The reasons are obvious. Any country using nuclear blackmail would be condemned by the whole world. More important, no one could be sure that carrying out such a threat would not trigger world War Three.

And, as Chernobyl reminded us, fallout knows no frontiers. The blackmailers would poison themselves.

5 'Only the Bomb stops the Russians from invading Western Europe'

You don't have to believe the Russians are pacifists to disagree with this.

What would the Russians gain by taking over Western Europe? They already have problems in Eastern Europe, without taking on ours as well.

But even if they wanted, they couldn't. There is no Soviet superiority, either of nuclear weapons or conventional forces. Experts agree that 'the conventional overall balance is still such as to make general military aggression a highly risky undertaking for either side'. (*The Military Balance*, 1985–6, Institute of Strategic Studies, London.)

6 'Only by being strong can we get the Russians to bargain with us'

'Star Wars' was supposed to bring the Russians back to negotiations, but it turned out to be the main thing preventing an agreement.

To use weapons as bargaining chips you must be willing to bargain them away. But no new weapons system has ever been bargained away in the history of the nuclear arms race.

British nuclear weapons could trigger the end of the world. But they are only a tiny fraction of the superpower arsenals. Even with nuclear weapons, Britain doesn't get a place at the nuclear conference table.

7 'Nuclear disarmament would split NATO and let our allies down'

Already seven of the sixteen NATO countries refuse to have nuclear weapons on their soil.

A non-nuclear Britain could work with other independently-minded countries in all parts of Europe. We could start to undo the senseless hostility between East and West.

And Britain could join with nuclear-free countries all over the world in pressing America and Russia to make real progress towards disarmament.

British nuclear disarmament doesn't mean opting out. It means playing a more active and independent role in world affairs.

We in Britain can still make a difference. It's time we did.

The view of Families for Defence:

NATO's Future At Stake

DO YOU KNOW THAT:

NATO's deterrent policy involves both nuclear and conventional forces. These are complementary. No amount of nuclear forces will be credible unless they are supported by adequate conventional forces. But conventional forces alone could never withstand a determined attack on Western Europe by vastly superior Soviet forces.

DO YOU KNOW THAT:

NATO's nuclear deterrent is indispensible to our defence. It constitutes an element of very great stability in East/West relations. The Soviet Union knows full well that it is a line which it must not cross except at the risk of the most appalling consequences.

DO YOU KNOW THAT:

Proposals for one-sided nuclear disarmament are unrealistic and dangerous. The Soviet leaders have made it clear that they would not follow suit.

DO YOU KNOW THAT:

One-sided abolition of Britain's independent nuclear deterrent, and the demand for the withdrawal of all U.S. nuclear forces based in this country, would bring about the disintegration of NATO.

It is clear that to end Britain's role as a nuclear power would be seen by the Soviets as a sign of weakness. It would deprive us of the ultimate guarantee of our freedom. It would leave France as the sole Western European nuclear power.

It is highly probably that, if pressed to withdraw their nuclear forces from this country, the USA would proceed to make massive reductions in their conventional forces in Europe. Western Europe and the USA would be effectively decoupled. Without the USA defence of the West is impossible.

It is certain that, confronted with a policy of one-sided nuclear disarmament by Britain, the European members of NATO (with the exception of France) would be both militarily weakened and politically destabilised. There would be strong internal pressures in our European Allies for neutralisation and non-alignment.

DO YOU KNOW THAT:

The Soviet military threat against Western Europe is today greater than ever. Their nuclear and conventional forces are superior in both numbers and fire power to those of the West. In these circumstances, it makes sense for Britain to continue to make an effective contribution to Western defence including the nuclear deterrent.

At present some 1.5% of Britain's defence budget is devoted to the independent nuclear deterrent. During its peak the TRIDENT programme will absorb some 3% of the defence budget – or 6% of the equipment budget – but will still cost proportionately less than certain current British defence equipment programmes. By comparison, France devotes some 10% of its defence budget to its nuclear forces.

DO YOU KNOW THAT:

Any plan to replace the British nuclear deterrent with improved conventional forces would involve very large increases in the size of those forces, enormous re-equipment programmes and expenditure vastly in excess of the cost of the nuclear forces.

DO YOU KNOW THAT:

By sending the wrong political signals to the Soviet Union at this time we are likely to lessen – not increase – the chances of a successful outcome to current East/West disarmament negotiation. The Soviets would attempt to exploit divisive Western policies.

DO YOU KNOW THAT:

Security and peace can, in the long term, only be better ensured by multilateral disarmament and balanced force reductions with each stage of the process open to verification. This is a long and slow business but it is one in which both West and East must persist and which all of us must support wholeheartedly.

DO YOU KNOW THAT:

Despite abhorrence of all nuclear weapons, in today's world there is really no realistic alternative to the present NATO policy of deterrence, if the West wishes to continue to live in both freedom and peace.

Activities

The leaflet extracts on the previous pages present two opposing points of view on nuclear weapons. On one side, the Families For Defence *(FFD) leaflet expresses support for Britain's possession of nuclear weapons and for its membership of NATO. On the other side, the* Campaign For Nuclear Disarmament *(CND) leaflet objects both to nuclear weapons and to organisations like NATO which support these weapons. The activities below will help you to understand the points of view presented in the two leaflets and then to argue your own views.*

Vocabulary

Check first that you understand the terms and vocabulary used in the nuclear weapons debate. Most of the terms below are used in one or both of the two leaflets, so discuss the meaning of:

NATO	*Star Wars*
Deterrence	*Pacifism*
Independent nuclear deterrent	*Neutralisation*
Unilateral disarmament	*Non-alignment*
Multilateral disarmament	*Verification.*
The Cold War	

Discussion and understanding

Read each leaflet through carefully, at least twice, so that you understand both the general points and the individual vocabulary terms used. Then in pairs or small groups, discuss the following questions, making notes of your answers.

1 Both FFD and CND say they have the same aim – freedom and peace. Broadly, how does each organisation say this aim can be brought about?

2 The CND leaflet makes seven title statements which it describes as 'myths'.
   – What do you understand by the word 'myth'?
   – Why have CND chosen to use this word?
   – What is the significance of the title, 'Seven Deadly Myths . . .'?

3 The FFD leaflet makes nine statements each beginning with the question, 'Do you know that . . . ?' Carefully compare FFD's nine statements with CND's seven. How many of FFD's statements would be described by CND as 'myths'?

4 Find at least six main points of disagreement between FFD and CND. Use a chart like the one opposite to show the contrast in their points of view:

FFD	CND
1. The Soviet military threat against the West is greater than ever before – they have superior nuclear and conventional forces ...	1. The Soviets are not a threat to the West as they have no military superiority either in nuclear or conventional forces ...

5   Compare the presentation and lay-out of the two leaflets.
    – How has each leaflet chosen to present its points of view?
    – Which method is the more effective and why?
    – Which leaflet uses the clearer page lay-out? Why do you think this?

6   Both leaflets were printed in 1987. Do you consider that the argument used by either 'side' has become less valid in the light of recent events?

Class discussion

This activity suggests a way of preparing for an informal class discussion of a contentious subject.

'Proposals for one-sided nuclear disarmament are unrealistic and dangerous.' (FFD)

'With defence policies based on nuclear weapons, we are gambling with life on earth.' (CND)

1   Select *one* of the argument statements above, or one similar.

2   Divide your class roughly in two – those in support of the statement, and those against it. Within your 'half', form small working groups.

3   As a group, prepare all the points you can think of in defence of your view. Always find reasons or known facts to back each point – an opinion which is unsubstantiated proves nothing! Then think of the points the other 'half' of the class may attack you with. Decide how you will argue against *their* points. (There should be a time limit of, say, 30 minutes for this stage in the exercise.)

4   Select one strong-minded person (not necessarily your teacher) to 'chair' the class discussion. The golden rule: If you want to speak, let the chairperson know by raising your hand; then wait until you are asked to speak. Don't just interrupt!

Writing

Choose one of the two statements above and write an argument essay, arguing the case *for* or *against* this view. (See *Techniques*: 'Drafting an argument essay'.)

Drafting an argument essay

Read this section to help you draft, edit and write an argument essay.

In an *argument essay*, you put forward the case *for* one side of an argument and also show why you think people who support the opposing side, are wrong.

Remember that a *discussion essay* asks for *both* sides of the case to be presented and may not necessarily require you to give your own opinion until the end. (See *Techniques*: 'Drafting a discussion essay', chapter 3.) But in an argument essay, you put forward your own views and defend them.

If you are going to write an argument essay, follow the advice given for this example:

'Proposals for one-sided nuclear disarmament are unrealistic and dangerous.'

Argue the case for or against this view.

Stage 1   Content

1   Use any notes you have gathered from class discussion to help you prepare your thoughts. Think carefully about what the essay title wants you to do and decide which 'side' of the argument you support.

2   Now prepare the points which support your view. To help you do this, divide a sheet of rough paper in two. In the *left*-hand column, note down at least three main points which support your view and give your reasons. Leave several lines blank between each point noted. Do the same for the *right*-hand column, this time noting down points the other 'side' may attack you with. Then give reasons why each of these points is unjustified in your view. For instance notes by a CND supporter might look like this:

For one-sided disarmament	Against deterrence
1. One sided disarmament is essential for defusing the world tension caused by the build up of nuclear weapons. This is because ...	1. 'One-sided disarmament is unrealistic because the two main nuclear powers would not follow suit.' Wrong: It would be realistic if Britain were to join other non-nuclear countries to put pressure on the nuclear powers to disarm...

3 Go back to each point in turn and think how you can give it more authority. You may be able to do this by:
- explaining and giving reasons why you think each point is justified;
- giving examples or illustrations: from your own and other people's experience, from information given by experts in the field, surveys, newspapers or books on the subject and from past or current events.

Stage 2   Structure

You can now turn your list of points into a first draft. The number of paragraphs in your essay will depend partly on how much you have to say. A full treatment of your subject may look something like this:

Paragraph 1/ Introduction :   Briefly give your point of view on the statement in the essay title. Perhaps say how the essay will present your case.

Paragraph 2 :   Give your first point from the *left*-hand column of your rough notes – that is, explaining and defending your point of view. Follow this with reasons and examples if appropriate.

Paragraphs 3–5 :   Start a new paragraph for each new main point which defends and develops your argument. Be sure that each new paragraph/point is clearly indicated by a marker: e.g. 'My third reason for attacking the statement in the title is . . .' *or*, 'Thirdly, I believe . . .'

Paragraphs 6–7 :   Give points from the *right*-hand column of your rough notes, with reasons why the other side's views are wrong.

Paragraph 8/ Conclusion :   Give a short statement summarising what you feel the essay has shown.

Stage 3   Editing

When you have written the first draft, examine it by asking yourself the questions below. When you feel that your essay satisfies the first question, move on to the second. It may also be helpful to get a friend to read your work through as a check on any of the following:

1   Does the argument develop logically through the essay, point by point?

2   Does each new paragraph indicate that it is making a new point?

3   Are all the points explained clearly, so that each one makes good sense and fits into your argument?

4   Is your vocabulary accurate and appropriate? (Underline any words you feel could be improved. Find a better word by doing any of the following: consulting someone; using a dictionary; using a Thesaurus.)

5   Have you checked your use of spelling, punctuation and grammar?

Stage 4   Writing

Now write the final version
of your argument essay.

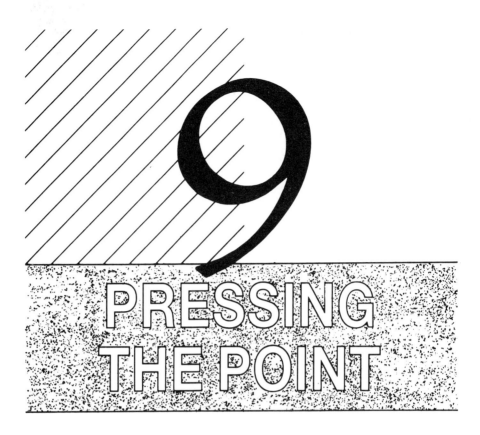

9

PRESSING THE POINT

SLOGANS

Famous slogans

The real thing.
COCA COLA

Beanz meanz Heinz.
—— **HEINZ** ——

Don't say brown
– say Hovis.
HOVIS

Heineken
refreshes the parts
other beers can not reach.
HEINEKEN

From Ssssch … you know who.
SCHWEPPES

Things happen after a Badedas bath.
BADEDAS

Persil washes whiter!
PERSIL WASHING POWDER

Your country needs you!
1ST WORLD WAR RECRUITMENT

Milk has gotta lotta bottle.
MILK

Guinness
is good for you.
GUINNESS

Well,
they said anything could happen.
SMIRNOFF VODKA

The Ultimate
Driving Machine.
BMW CARS

Recent slogans

Try to match the slogans to their products.

Anybody can make a mistake.

Keep in touch.

No white lies.

Free the spirit.

Some girls are simply smoother than others.

Behind a successful man, you'll find an elegant lady.

It's gentle. That's its strength.

Significant moments.

Leave the heavies to battle it out.

PERSIL

SAMSON
tobacco

NISSAN
cars

OMEGA
watches

BRAUN
leg-shavers

PERNOD
drink

ROYAL MAIL

TIPPEX

MINI METRO

Oral work

1 Selling an object

In pairs, try to 'sell' something in a time limit of, say, two minutes. You could 'sell' anything available: a bag, an item of stationery or clothing, a book, or bring something into the class you really would like to sell! Your aim is to convince your potential buyer that he or she really needs the item you are trying to sell.

After this, see if one or two people will volunteer to sell their item to someone in the class. If one of you *is* prepared to buy the item for sale within the time limit, then the sales technique is likely to have been successful!

Then, as a class, work out what were the selling techniques used.

2 Selling a point of view

This time try to 'sell' a point of view – something you feel strongly about. Preferably pair with someone who is either indifferent to your point of view or disagrees with it. Your topic might be vegetarianism, homework, the exam system, blood sports, smoking or whatever. Within a time limit, try to convince your partner that you are right. Then, if you are brave, try to convince your class.

3 Slogans

Read through the famous slogans at the beginning of the chapter, then discuss:
– Which of these famous slogans are still used today?
– Select two or three slogans you like. Can you explain why they are effective, in your view? Can you recall any other famous slogans?
– Why do you think advertisers use slogans?
– Take any three products from the list of famous slogans. Come up with a new winning slogan for each product.

Now look at the recent slogans for well-known products.
– Can you fit each slogan to the right product?
– Which other products could the slogan be advertising? Explain why you think this.
– Do you think any of the recent slogans will last?
– From your study of both the famous and the recent slogans, draw out some general principles about what makes a good advertising slogan: e.g. 'A slogan should be short . . .'

The only class system you'll encounter when you join the force.

When you join the police, it's not who you know but what you know that counts.

To us, your social background doesn't mean a thing. We're not influenced by the colour of your skin or your accent.

All we want to know is, have you got what it takes to become a good police officer?

Have you got the strength of character, can you communicate with people, most importantly, can you listen and learn?

We'll find this out in your first two years of training, both in the classroom and on the street.

We'll help you develop from a raw recruit to a fully fledged police constable.

After that, promotion through the ranks is based on your performance.

If you have the ambition, you can go as far as your professional ability will take you.

We're looking for men and women from all sections of the community over the age of 18½. Ideally you'll be at least 172cms tall if you're a man, 162cms for a woman, and have five 'O' levels, but your personal qualities are just as important.

TO FIND OUT MORE RING: 01-725 4492 (ANSAPHONE: 725 4575). OR WRITE TO: THE RECRUITING OFFICER, THE METROPOLITAN POLICE, CAREERS INFORMATION CENTRE, DEPT. MD 734, NEW SCOTLAND YARD, LONDON SW1H 0BG.

THE EARTH'S LIFE SUPPORT SYSTEMS ARE FAILING.

One of the Earth's vital organs is collapsing: the rainforests are being hacked down at a rate of 100 acres a minute.

Within a single generation, there will be virtually no tropical rainforest left on Earth.

Disastrous roads-to-nowhere are destroying Amazonia. The loggers and bankers will make a quick killing, but they won't replant. The ranchers and slash-and-burn farmers will get a few years' poor grazing or stunted crops. And then, like Ethiopia, the land will die.

But we are not powerless. Add your strength to the pressure group leading the campaign to make the timber industry, governments, and The World Bank think again about destroying the rainforest.

We need your contributions now, let the forests live, let the Earth breathe.

HELP THE EARTH FIGHT BACK.

I support Friends of the Earth's fight to save our Tropical Rainforests.

TR0A

Name_____

Address_____

_____ Post Code_____

Please enrol me as a supporter, and send me your quarterly newspaper. I enclose £12 ☐

I enclose a donation of £500 ☐ £50 ☐ £25 ☐ £10 ☐ Other ☐

And I would like to receive your Tropical Rainforest Action Pack.

Send to Friends of the Earth Ltd, FREEPOST, Mitcham, Surrey, CR4 9AR. No stamp needed.

FRIENDS OF THE EARTH

Why should he care which credit card you use?

Children like Sam need your help.

They need it now, and they need it badly.

Which is why your choice of credit card could be vital.

Because the new Bank of Scotland NSPCC Visa Card has been created with a particular object in mind.

To help children.

Children in need, in danger, and distress.

Last year, the NSPCC helped over 44,000 youngsters.

To some that meant the difference between life and death.

Which is why we've joined forces.

And why we're asking for your support.

For every one of these new Visa accounts opened, we'll donate £5 to the NSPCC.

But it goes a lot further than that.

Whenever you buy something with the card, you'll help the children too.

It's a splendid way of contributing.

You don't have to get into debt, or run up credit.

You don't even have to use your card more than you usually do.

Because every penny counts.

And with lots of people taking part, the sums will soon mount up.

They could easily top the million pound mark.

That's an awful lot of hope.

For very little effort.

So whether or not you already have a credit card, please return the coupon now.

 **BANK OF SCOTLAND**
A FRIEND FOR LIFE NSPCC *VISA*

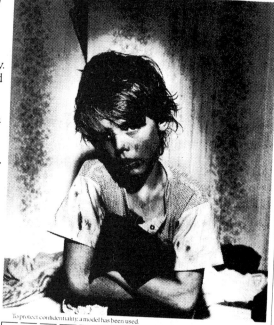

To protect confidentiality, a model has been used.

Please send me an application form and full written details of the new Bank of Scotland NSPCC Visa Card. I am over 18 years of age. Send to: Bank of Scotland Visa Centre, FREEPOST, Dunfermline, Fife KY99 5BR; or dial 100 and ask for FREEFONE Bank of Scotland.

First names _____
(Mr/Mrs/Miss/Ms)

Surname _____

Address _____

_____

_____

_____

FG/880322

Postcode _____ Tel. No. _____

Cardholders in England, Wales and Northern Ireland will benefit the NSPCC and, in Scotland, the RSSPCC

160

Discussion and understanding

Please read Techniques: *'Analysing adverts' before working on these activities. This will give you some theoretical understanding of the special ways advertisements can work to persuade people to buy something.*

Read through the four advertisements on the previous pages. Then, in pairs or small groups, select *one* of these adverts to study in more detail, using the questions below. Make sure though, that *all four* adverts are studied amongst the class. Then, later on, the class as a whole can compare the different approaches of the four adverts.

1   Who is the advertiser? How does the advert signify the organisation it is representing?

2   For whom is the advert intended? Is it aimed at a broad or a narrow range of people and how do you know? Note down all the indications the advert gives you as to the range and type of people for whom it is intended.

3   What does the advert want its audience to do?

4   Study how the advert tries to persuade its audience to do what it wants. Make notes on the following selling techniques:

   Product : how does the advert promote the features of the product, profession, service or membership?
   Audience : how does the advert appeal to people's needs or feelings?
   Impact : how are the images and language of the advert itself used to persuade people? (See example on p. 165.)

Writing

Design a newspaper or magazine advertisement for *one* of the following:

a unisex deodorant	*a student 'help-line'*
a diet drink	*a charity*
a pair of jeans	*a local youth training scheme.*
a guide to passing an examination	

   Your advert may include some or all of these elements as appropriate: a slogan or caption, an illustration or photograph, persuasive text, the advertiser's name, address, company logo, and a form to fill in.

   Make your advert as persuasive as possible, drawing on a range of appropriate selling techniques.

Analysing adverts

This section will help you both to study the advertisements on the previous pages, and to design and write a similar type of advertisement yourself.

The main purpose of advertising is to persuade a particular group of people to buy something. Usually advertising is associated with selling a product – like a washing machine to busy housewives. But adverts can also sell less tangible things. For example:

- a service : for banking, insurance, equipment hire, 'help-lines'
- a membership : to 'pressure' groups, clubs, charities
- a profession : job or training vacancies, career opportunities.

In order to understand how successful advertisements work, you will need to ask yourself some questions about the way they are designed.

1 Advertiser

Who is the advertiser?

An advertisement may signify the company, group or person it is representing by one or more of the following means:

a logo or insignia   *a slogan*
a name   *a distinctive image, and/or colour.*
an address

- Think of two or three famous brands of products, like soft drinks, jeans or perfume. Then work out how the company identifies itself in its adverts. Remember that for really famous products, the company doesn't need to give its own name – the brand name of the product is sufficient.

2 Audience (or client)

For whom is the advert intended?

Many adverts are aimed at a 'target audience' – that is, specified groups of people, who have been identified as potential clients. An advertiser may have to carry out research to define this 'target audience' by considering such factors as:

age
sex
socio-economic background
education
viewing habits : e.g. magazines/television/train posters?
perceived 'needs' : e.g. for financial security, health and fitness, a job with career prospects.

- An advert will have ways of identifying its intended audience, indicating who is included and who is excluded. Think of any well-known advert currently on television. How does this signify the type of people for whom it is intended?

3 Message

What is the advert saying?

In many cases, adverts are saying little more than 'buy this'. A variation of this – in the case of charitable and political causes – may be 'give generously' or 'join us'. Some businesses also want their adverts to put across a certain image e.g. British Gas and its 'Building a better Britain' campaign. In all cases, an advertiser's powers of persuasion have to be convincing because there are so many competitors trying to sell similar products, services, causes and images.

4 Selling techniques

What are the ways in which an advert persuades people to buy?

The techniques advertisers use have become increasingly sophisticated and only an outline of these, as they apply to magazine and newspaper advertising, can be given here.

There are three main types of technique:

'Product centred' techniques

These are selling techniques which concentrate on the product, service, membership or whatever it is that is to be sold. They praise its particular *features*. In the case of a washing machine, for example, these might be:
- cheap purchase price
- high standard of design
- speedy performance
- reliability
- service and parts guarantee
- wide choice of 'washing programmes'
- economical to run.

- Think of an example of: a product / a service / a job or career / a club membership in which you or a friend have a personal interest. Think of the selling features associated with each one.

'Audience centred' techniques

These are selling techniques which concentrate on the advertiser's view of the 'needs' of the target audience. Such 'needs' may often be *desires* for things which are not strictly necessary to people's daily existence – such as the desire for a better life style. The advertiser's skill is to persuade people that a desire *is* a need, which their product can meet. These 'needs' may exist on two levels:

practical 'needs' :   such as more time, more money.

psychological 'needs' :   such as the need/desire for financial security, a
                             more sophisticated life style, good health, good
                             looks or self-confidence. Also deeper feelings,
                             such as guilt and the desire for a clear
                             conscience, fears for the future, etc.

- To which particular 'needs' in people, may the following appeal?

  A pension scheme   *A pair of Levis.*
  Face make-up   *A sports car*
  Joining the RAF   *Membership of a political party.*

'Impact centred' techniques:

These are selling techniques which use the impact of both visual
presentation and language to help sell something.

Judge whether an advert will make an effective impact on its target
audience by considering these important design rules:

Visual presentation : – the overall lay-out of caption, picture and text
                           should be clear and pleasing to the eye.
                         – the choice of picture/images should tell you
                           instantly what the advert is about.
                         – the use of picture/images should be striking.
                         – the typeface should be readable and pleasing to
                           look at.

Language use :   – the reading level (i.e. the choice of vocabulary,
                           sentence length and so on) should be appropriate
                           for the age and understanding of the target
                           audience.
                         – the text should be persuasive without being
                           'pushy'. It may use any of the following features:

                         Wit : witty or clever language such as puns (jokes on
                           words with double meanings), or comparisons to
                           amuse and entertain the audience.

                         Chattiness : friendly and informal tone and style to
                           make contact with the audience.

                         Emotiveness : words or phrases which provoke an
                           emotional reaction in the audience.

                         Forcefulness : strong or violent-sounding words or
                           phrases, again to provoke an audience reaction.

5 Response

What does the advert hope to achieve?

In most cases, what is hoped for is clearly an audience response to the
message. If the message is 'please join us', then the advert must provide a
way for people to do so.

Many adverts do not necessarily expect a measurable response. For
example, making a target audience aware of the brand name of a new
product and what it does, is often the most an advert can do.

An analysis

How does this advertisement persuade you to send money to the Blue Cross charity?

PHOTOGRAPHIC RECONSTRUCTION

HUSHED PUPPIES.

✝

These poor little chaps were dumped in a shoe-box and callously left to die in a wood.

When the Blue Cross found them they were on their last legs, barely able to utter a whimper.

We're a charity that cares for sick or injured animals or those made homeless through no fault of their own.

After a little loving care and attention, the pups were soon back to their mischievous selves and placed in a secure new home.

However, to keep this much needed service going, we depend entirely on your support. So please help by filling in the coupon below.

I'd like more information on Blue Cross ☐   I'd like to make a donation ☐
I enclose my cheque/postal order for £ _____

Name _____

Address _____

_____ Postcode _____

To: Blue Cross Animals Hospital,
1 Hugh St., Victoria, London SW1V 1QQ.   **BLUE✚CROSS**

DE. 24.6.f

Picture: two puppies in a cardboard box.

- Indicates the work of the Blue Cross – caring for sick animals.
- An emotive image: two pups in cramped, sordid conditions – not a basket but an old shoe box. Signifies maltreatment perhaps? The pups' eyes are shut: are they alive or dead?
- 'Photographic reconstruction': the picture looks real but in fact it has been 'reconstructed'. Might this reinforce the caring image of the Blue Cross – caring for the animals first, publicising later?

Caption: pun on 'Hushed Puppies'.

- Echoes the picture of the shoe box – Hush Puppy shoes. Have the pups been discarded like old shoes?
- Plays on the word 'hushed' with its other meaning of 'silenced' or 'killed'.

Text

- Emotive language:
  'poor little chaps': the pups are made to sound human;
  'barely able to utter a whimper';
  'on their last legs': the weakness and frailty of the pups is stressed;
- Forceful language:
  'callously left to die': cruelty of people responsible is stressed;
  'depend entirely on your support': the reader is also made to feel responsible – an appeal to the reader's conscience.
- Story-telling style:
  the story has a happy ending but it also has a moral.

Form

- An emotional response is anticipated, so a form is supplied for immediate action.

Logo: A cross

- Connotations of the Christian cross: charity and good works.
- Also the Red Cross charity: nursing and care.

10 HEADING ON

TRAVELLING ON YOUR OWN

A Travel Survival Kit

This article was written by a tertiary college teacher for her students. Pauline Leonard lived abroad for several years and in that time travelled widely.

For some of you, this summer may be the first time you set out on your own to travel – in this country or abroad. It is said that travel broadens the mind, but if you fail to take a few basic precautions, it can become a miserable, disappointing or even frightening experience leading to narrow, bitter perceptions of all things foreign. Here are a few tips to help you avoid some of the hazards and pitfalls of cheap holidaying.

Before you go

It is a good idea to do some research on the places you intend to visit before you go, as this will help you to plan what to take with you. I strongly recommend buying a good, all-purpose guide book – the 'Lonely Planet' series is excellent, or the 'Shoestring' guides to cheap travelling. Things to check are:

1 Documentation

If you are travelling abroad, make sure that your passport is up to date – it can take several weeks to get a new one. Any enquiries should go to your nearest Passport office. Also find out whether you will need a visa. If you do, contact the country's Embassy or Consulate (listed in London telephone directories) for information. An international student identity card (ISIC) is proof of your student status and makes you eligible for many discounts. These are available from Transalpino or Worldwide Student Travel.

2 Getting there

Your options are air, coach, train, cycling or walking! Air travel is the most expensive with the drawbacks that you can't stop en route and you may still need to pay for extra transport once you're there. Coach and train do a number of cheap deals for students. If you're thinking of taking a bicycle to Europe, you must know your destination and send the bike separately by train as baggage, well in advance. Find out more from the Student Travel Association or Worldwide Student Travel.

3 Accommodation

Camping is probably the cheapest especially if you take your own tent. The national tourist office of the country you are visiting will give you details of campsites. Youth hostelling is also inexpensive and saves you the effort of carrying camping equipment on your back. You will need to become a member of the Youth Hostel Association to get hostel lists and maps for the relevant countries. But it is usually safe not to bother booking accommodation before you go – in fact it is often better to judge what is available once you are there and also this gives you complete freedom to move on. As long as you aim to get to your destination by early afternoon, you should find somewhere. Head straight for the local tourist office who will give you addresses, maps and guide books.

4 Weather

Be sensible about your own tolerance level to extremes of temperature. If you're not good in hot weather, then try to avoid Southern Europe in July and August. Sweating along a hot, dusty road weighed down by a full pack with no hope of a campsite or hostel for miles in sweltering temperatures is *not* fun and threatens to wreck the most harmonious of friendships! If you're camping, check the night time temperature – many hot countries get very cold at night and you will need a warm sleeping-bag and sweater.

5 Clothing

The important thing is not to take too much – and to take a range. Obviously, the weather is an important factor to consider, but you should also check out religious and moral attitudes and anticipate the kind of sight-seeing and travelling you will be doing. In Indonesia, my husband ended up borrowing one of my skirts – as shorts are not considered suitable clothing in Hindu temples! Women especially need to have clothes with which to cover shoulders, arms and legs as there are places of cultural interest in many parts of the world, which expect this token of 'respect'. Remember, if you're likely to be doing much walking or travelling by bus or train, comfortable clothes are crucial.

6 Luggage

Try and take as little as possible, whilst anticipating most of your needs. With clothes, just take one or two of everything and wash them as you travel around. Remember, you will have to carry your own bag – sometimes for long distances. If you plan to walk a lot, a light-weight rucksack is essential.

7 Money

Your budget will guide what you can afford to take with you. If you have little money, then you probably won't be able to eat out very often – and this may mean taking cooking equipment with you. However don't cut things so fine that you can't afford to eat properly. You'll find yourself roaming the streets forlornly staring into restaurant windows. Try and talk to someone who has already been to the country before you go, and seek their advice on likely costs. It is better to go for a shorter time that you *can* afford than a longer time that you can't. Remember too that you should always carry your money and documents in a safe place – a money belt, or a pocket slung around the neck or sewn into your clothes.

8 Provisions

Generally you will be able to buy everyday provisions in most countries in the world. I have found that it is better to buy these things or do without, rather than lug around huge packets of Daz or jars of Marmite 'just in case'. Remember, a holiday is all about change – and so it may do you good to go without Golden Wonder crisps for a while. However, water-purifying tablets, mosquito-bite cream, and a first-aid kit are sensible additions which don't take up much room. You're bound to get some sort of tummy upset, so be prepared!

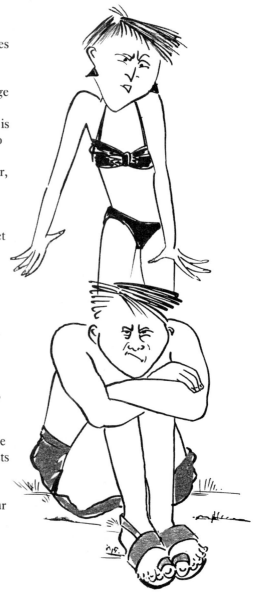

9 Company

If you are intending to travel with others, then choose people with whom you feel at ease. This may seem obvious, but friendships are tested considerably when travelling, as you have to cope with decision making and being in each other's company constantly. Go with people who share your outlook and interests and with whom you can be honest, open and relaxed. Humour is the most important quality you and your travelling companions will need!

Once you're there

Be adventurous whilst being sensible. Try to experience the local culture, eat the local food in small cafes, and use public transport. Being open, friendly and talkative can be extremely rewarding, in terms of both friendships and learning about other cultures. I have attended the initiation ceremony of a Buddhist monk, visited a private Greek island, seen crocodiles in deserted mangroves and joined in a Japanese tea ceremony – all from chatting to people on buses or in cafes.

Eating the local food can be fun

Postscript

The thought of travel is often more daunting than the activity itself. Once you're off, it's amazing how smoothly things go. If small problems do arise, they're often part of the fun and the experience. Talk to as many knowledgeable people as you can – and then go!

Pauline Leonard

Instructive writing

Write your own guide on the lines of 'A Travel Survival Kit'. Choose one of the following options:

1 A guide to your local area

Write a guide for foreign students who may be visiting your area 'on the cheap'. Although it can be assumed that they have a reasonable understanding of English, make your guide as clear and straightforward as possible. It may be useful to visit your local tourist office to pick up some leaflets about your district, but the idea is that you write a guide 'by a student' based on your *own* experience and knowledge. Organise your material under such sections as:

– Places to visit
– Places to stay
– Entertainment
– Ways of getting about
– Places to eat and drink

(In each section, aim to compare the cost of things and to estimate how your reader would get the best value for money.)

2 A guide to an 'adventure' holiday

Write a guide to a 'hobby' or 'adventure' holiday you have experienced in this country or abroad. The guide could be for other students from your college or school, who may have an interest in this type of holiday. Examples of titles may be, 'A guide to . . .':

Camping on Dartmoor
Pony trekking in the Brecon Beacons
Orienteering in the Lake District

Sailing off the East coast
Skiing at Aviemore.

The aim of this guide is that it should allow readers who may be thinking of going on a similar type of holiday to benefit from your own experience. Organise your material under such headings as:

– Purpose of holiday
– Skills/qualities you must have
– Cost
– Clothing
– Equipment
– Accommodation and Food
– Safety precautions
– Social life
– Weather
– What you will learn.

3 'A guide to a holiday in . . .'

Write a guide to spending a holiday in any place you have visited, which you found interesting – either in this country or abroad. You may need to refresh your mind about this holiday by studying maps, photo albums, brochures and guide books. But the aim is to advise other young people how to get the best from 'a holiday in . . .' by drawing on *your* experience. Organise your material under a series of headings, using 'A Travel Survival Kit' as your model.

Writing a summary

As a member of the editorial team of your college or sixth form magazine 'Help Yourself', you have been asked to submit a short article for the end-of-year edition. The team have decided to do a double-page 'pull-out' on the subject of cheap student travel abroad. One page will not be your concern – dealing with the comparative costs of transport to and from the continent. But the other page *will* be left to you – a brief guide to 'surviving' a holiday abroad. As no one in the magazine's team has travelled abroad on their own yet, you are relying on a rather long article by a teacher. You have been sent this memo from the editor giving you some advice about how to write your own article:

From: The Editor: 'Help Yourself'

Subject: Article – A Travel Survival Guide

We'd like you to write an article of no longer than 500 words, using the same information as Pauline Leonard's article, but condensing it so that you just give the main points. The idea is that students can read your article through quickly, but still get the important information.

1 Include all the sections except the ones entitled, 'Documentation' and 'Getting there' – they'll be dealt with on the other page. Keep your introduction and conclusion to a minimum.

2 Cut out all the chat – the 'my husband and I' stuff. It's amusing in its way, but not relevant to us.

3 Write in whole sentences – we don't want this in note form – but keep the sentences crisp and to the point!

4 Address the reader as 'you', like the Leonard article. Although you are having to summarise, make sure your article sounds friendly.

5 Include a sketch of the lay-out, if this is not obvious in the draft you submit to us.

I'll look forward to receiving your article as soon as possible. Don't forget our deadline!

Thanks!

GIVING A TALK

There may be only a few occasions in your life when you need to give a formal talk unless of course you intend to become an actor, a teacher, a politician, a television personality or take on a similar public role. But in many jobs with a level of responsibility, and even in some social activities there may be times when you are asked to talk to a group of people.

Few people are born speakers. Most learn the skills needed with practice, and even experienced speakers may find giving a talk nerve-wracking. But preparing your talk in advance, as well as learning a few basic techniques in giving a talk, will certainly increase your confidence and improve your performance.

To help you achieve this, you will find the following guidelines useful.

Thinking

Once you have a topic, allow yourself time to think about it:

1 Let ideas for the talk come to you naturally, while you are doing other things.

2 Discuss your initial thoughts with someone – a friend, your teacher, your parents. Remember to note down any particularly good ideas as they occur to you.

3 Read books, newspapers and magazines on the topic of your talk.

Planning

A talk must have a structure and a sense of direction, like any piece of written work. Working to a planned outline will not only help you to prepare the talk, but also will help your audience to follow and enjoy the topic. If you have not been given an outline, you will need to plan one yourself, along these lines:

1 Note down all the main points you think your talk should cover. To do this, ask yourself what the aim of the talk is and what the audience may hope to learn. Consider also your own areas of knowledge and expertise on the topic – that is, what you are *able* to talk about.

2 Review your list of points, grouping them under headings and assembling these in an order which is logical and shows a sense of direction.

For example, if you are talking about a hobby, you may choose to use a simple time structure:

Past experience ➤➤➤ Present involvement ➤➤➤ Future hopes

If you are putting forward an argument, then your structure may look like this:

Presentation of one main point:
a reasons ⎫
b illustrations ⎬ repeat this formula as necessary
c reply to objections ⎭

3 Whatever the topic, you will need a striking way of opening and closing your talk.

Your opening should be original and interesting – enough to make people want to hear what you have to say. Apart from the standard but dull approach of giving your aim and an outline of the talk, other tactics to consider are:
– asking a question;
– telling a story or an anecdote;
– using a quotation.

Your conclusion should not tail off but finish positively. The standard approach is a summary, but consider using one of the opening tactics as appropriate, or giving your audience a chance to participate by inviting them to comment.

4 Visual aids and/or hand-outs are useful in two ways. They can give your presentation some variety and, if you are nervous, they can give your audience something to look at other than yourself. Make sure though that the visual aids complement what you have to say and that their value is obvious. The usual aids are:

Black/whiteboard	*Posters*
Overhead projections	*Video-tapes*
Flipcharts	*Cassette-tapes*
Slides	*Props – e.g. equipment, souvenirs.*

Recalling

Once you have worked out a talk outline and noted down what you intend to say under each heading, you will need a way of recalling your points when you give the talk. The main methods are:

1 Learning the talk off by heart

This approach is not really recommended as it can produce a stilted, unnatural effect unless you are very practised at it.

2 Reading the talk from a sheet

Again this produces a dull and wooden talk, unless you are an experienced reader. It is only recommended for the very nervous!

3 Using summary headings

A series of cards or a sheet giving the main headings, any quotations, and facts and statistics in brief, at which you can glance from time to time, is the best method, providing you know your material!

Once you have selected a method of recalling your talk, make sure you practise – out loud, checking the timing and preferably using a tape-recorder. If you are using visual aids or hand-outs, make sure these are prepared well in advance and that you know how to use any equipment.

Giving the talk

The main thing is to try to relax, remembering that you are not putting on a performance but talking *to* people. It is worth trying to be aware of the following:

1 Body language

Your body may express the tension you feel and distract the audience from what you are saying. If you know that you are normally quite restless, it is particularly important that you try to relax and control the movements of your body. Here are a few guidelines:

Eye movement: Try to look at individual people in the room for a moment only, taking them in with a sweep of the eye. Avoid fixing one or two people with your gaze – this can be very off-putting! Also avoid staring fixedly at an object above people's heads. Unless you are speaking from a stage to a hallful of people, you may look very tense.

Gesture: Try to make arm and hand movements slow and sweeping, rather than quick and jerky. Gestures are important because they can add emphasis and expression to a point, but if gestures become fidgety, they may be very off-putting.

Posture: Sitting or standing, try to keep your body erect without becoming rigid. A slumped posture looks slovenly, whereas a straight one looks as if you are purposeful and controlled.

Movement: Unless you are giving a demonstration, keep movements to a minimum. Striding around may have some effect in a lecture theatre but in a smaller room, can upset an audience's concentration.

2 Spoken language

There are many features of your voice over which you may have little control – such as accent, pitch and timbre (the special quality and tone of your own voice). But there are other features which you *can* control, helping an audience to enjoy your talk more. These include:

Volume: Make sure people can hear what you are saying! Neither speak too softly nor let your voice boom. Usually, you will have to speak louder than you are accustomed to – try to imagine your voice 'touching' the four walls of the room. If you are in any doubt about whether everybody can hear you, ask them!

Clarity: Speak clearly, so that people can hear and understand each word. Never use a complex phrase where a simple one will do. Either explain or avoid using any technical jargon, which non-specialists will not understand.

Pace: A tendency with inexperienced speakers is to talk too fast. Make sure that you speak in a calm, measured way – people will pay far more attention to you. Also use pauses – before a surprise statement; before the punchline in a joke or funny story; when people are laughing at a witty comment; and when you wish to emphasise something.

Stress: Place a stress on words or phrases to which you would like your audience to pay particular attention.

Finally be good-humoured and enthusiastic – if you are stimulated by what you have to say, other people will be too!

Giving a talk

(For this activity, you may find it helpful to follow the guidance in Techniques: *'Giving a talk'.)*

Prepare and give a talk to your class lasting between 5 and 15 minutes on one of the following subjects.

1 A hobby, interest or expertise

For example:

A sport : a team game, sailing, riding, skiing, orienteering, martial arts, athletics.

Music : playing a musical instrument, playing in a group, singing.

Arts : dancing, painting, acting.

Membership : clubs, societies, charities, political groups.

Other : computer programming, cookery, record collecting, embroidery, training animals.

Suggestion: Look at why/how you became involved; what the activity involves in terms of skills, practice, time, cost, equipment, etc; your own triumphs and failures, your future involvement.

2 My future job/profession/career

For example:

nursing
computing
the Forces
child care
engineering
business.

Suggestion: Describe the career; its role in our society; what attracts you to it; why you may be suited; how you enter; future prospects.

3 'My views on . . .'

Give your views either for or against a subject you feel strongly about.
For example:

abortion   *nuclear energy*
bloodsports   *private v. state education*
equal opportunities   *violence on television*
exams   *vivisection*
human rights   *the welfare state.*
marriage

4 A holiday/travel

Use illustrations such as slides, posters and maps. For example:

A holiday with a group
A holiday abroad
An 'adventure' holiday
Travelling.

5 My favourite writer

Discuss your reasons for liking the work of a poet, playwright or author, by referring closely to their writing. Look at the writer's use of plot, characters, particular themes and language.

END-OF-TERM ACTIVITIES

The activities on these pages can be a creative and entertaining way of ending the term or year. All three activities can be video-taped effectively as 'television programmes'.

True or Bluff?

A good end-of-term activity is to play an adapted version of the television quiz programme, 'Call My Bluff'. If possible set up the activity as a television programme and video it.

Object of the game

In this panel game, two teams of three contestants compete to guess the meaning of little known and highly unusual words. Each team has prepared its own list of words using a good dictionary. For each word, one team presents two false but plausible sounding definitions ('bluffs') and one true definition to a contestant on the other team. This contestant must then use his/her wit and judgement to guess the true definition. The winning team, scoring the higher number of points, will be the one which is better able to distinguish true word definitions from false ones.

How to play

1   Each game has two teams of three people and one presenter. The presenter has a list of all the words from both teams, and then gives the members of the two teams their turn to guess a word in this order:

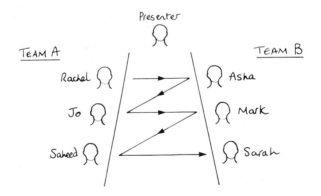

2 The game works in this way. Let's say Rachel in team A is given the word, *hurst*.

Asha defines it as : 'a car used in a funeral to carry a coffin from the funeral parlour to the cemetery, church or crematorium.'

Mark defines it as : 'a wood, thicket or copse frequently used in place names and also meaning a sand bank beside a river.'

Sarah defines it as : 'an Anglo-Saxon word meaning a primitive sort of cottage often rented by peasants on large country estates.'

Now Rachel must try to guess the correct definition. If she is right, the team B member with the correct definition will hold up a card saying *true* and Team A will win a point. If she is wrong, the team B member who gave the incorrect definition will hold up a card saying *bluff* and team B will win the point.

The second round follows in the same way, but this time Asha in Team B is offered a word, which Team A will then define.

How to prepare for the game

1 Your team will need one dictionary per person and should find somewhere to work, out of the earshot of the team against which you will be competing.

2 In your team, select a number of words. Try to select words which are completely unknown to you all but sound like other, more common words. This way, you may confuse people about a word's true meaning.

3 Now work out your definitions for each word. If there are to be a total of 12 words in the game, then your team will be responsible for devising a set of 3 definitions for each of 6 words – 18 definitions in all.

With the false definitions, try to make them sound as plausible (or indeed, as implausible) as the true definition. It may be helpful to 'raid' a dictionary for real definitions from other rare words – to make the false definitions more plausible. Remember that you can invent your own way of pronouncing all falsely defined words. The correct pronunciation will be given in the dictionary.

4 When your team has worked out the definitions, make a card for each word/definition like this:

Then distribute each set of word definitions between the team members, ensuring that each person has a mixture of *true* and *bluff* cards.

5 Spend some time 'learning' the definition you will give for each word, so that when you play the game, you speak out confidently and with some panache, glancing down at your card only if necessary.

6 If you choose to be a presenter, you have the following things to prepare:
   - Draw up the list of words for the game, alternating Team A and B words. (You will need to work with both teams to decide this order – but keep secret each team's choice of words.)
   - Work out how you will introduce the game: welcome viewers, give brief idea of the object and rules of the game and introduce the two teams of contestants; and also how you will conclude the game.
   - Decide on a way of exhibiting the word for each round and marking up the score for the audience to see.

Just a Minute

Object of the game

In this panel game, based on the radio programme of the same title, each contestant aims to speak continuously on a given subject for one full minute. In this time, the contestant speaking must not:
- *repeat* points or ideas, phrases or key words;
- *hesitate* in making the speech, by saying 'um' 'er' or pausing;
- *deviate* from the subject of the speech by talking about something which is not relevant to it.

How to play

1 The game is best played if there are two teams of three contestants and an adjudicator. If a member of Team A manages to speak continuously for one minute without repeating, hesitating or deviating, then he or she is awarded two points. If he or she is correctly challenged by a member of team B, then the challenger wins a point and takes over the speech for the time remaining. If that person finishes the speech unchallenged by Team A, he or she wins an extra point. On the occasions when an incorrect challenge is made, the speaker is awarded an extra point and carries on. All challenges are decided by the adjudicator. To summarise:
   - *2 points* : to a speaker for making a complete one-minute speech.
   - *1 point* : to an opponent making a correct challenge.
   - *1 point* : to a speaker who takes over and completes a speech.
   - *1 point* : to a speaker if incorrectly challenged.

2 Make sure that one person in the class has the sole job of operating a stop-watch. Remember that each time a speaker is interrupted, the watch must be stopped and the time remaining noted.

Some ideas for subjects

The Top Ten	*Table manners*
Computers	*Bad drivers*
No smoking	*April Fool's Day*
Saturday jobs	*Soap operas*
Superstition	*Breakfast*
Exams	*Sunday*
Money	*Qualities in a friend*
Sun-bathing	*Nicknames*

A breakfast television programme

Make a breakfast television programme, either for national or for local viewers. Divide your class into groups of 8–12 to make a programme each – perhaps from rival television channels. The aim of the programme will be to inform and entertain viewers at breakfast time.

Hold a meeting as a group to decide:

1 The editorial approach of the programme: decide whether the programme will have a light, 'magazine' approach or whether it will emphasize news and current affairs.

2 The programme content. Possible 'features' might be:

The day's news	*Interviews with famous people*
Weather	*Horoscopes*
Sport	*Problem letters*
Music	*The Arts:* film releases, books,
Political matters	exhibitions, theatre.

3 Jobs and responsibilities. Each of you may have to take on two types of work:
   – **Off-screen editorial work and script-writing:**
   Allocate one person to be programme editor who supervises the group's work and makes final decisions about the running order of 'features', time allocation for each feature and so on. This person should not do any 'on-screen presenting' (see below) – he or she will be busy enough!
   Allocate a pair of people to work on each 'feature' selected for the programme.

– **On-screen presenting and role play:**
    Allocate roles to the group. For example, who will be:
> *the main presenters*
> *the news reader*
> *the weather forecaster*
> *the people being interviewed*
> *presenters for specialist features* like music, sport, or medicine?

Do not try to be too ambitious as a group. Make your programme fairly short – somewhere between 10 and 20 minutes. Only select three or four separate features. If you are in charge of script-writing a feature, it makes sense for you to act in it. Bear in mind that all features have to be 'studio based' – there's no place for live film coverage! But studio interviews, news reports, advice from experts and so on is fine.